ATTENTION!!!

IMPORTANT legal notice to law enforcement and all third-parties pertaining to Search and Seizure

_____
Signature

_____
Print Name

ZuluShield

Firearms Legal Defense

Name		Book #	
Address			
Phone		Email	

Table of Contents

Introduction

To shoot or not to shoot is a question on the minds of all armed-professionals and armed-citizens alike. Many naively assume the answer will miraculously become unmistakably obvious when they're faced with a life or death situation. Most people even conclude that when faced with a Deadly Threat, they'll use 'Reason' to determine an appropriate course of action. Unfortunately, a person's decision to shoot is directly dependent upon their pre-programmed psychological Fight, Flight or Freeze Mechanism, meaning they'll react how they've been conditioned to react. What's worse, it's quite typically going be a decision completely absent any real cognitive process whatsoever. This means, there's no time to ponder and determine the most reasonable response for a given situation when 'Reasonableness' is exactly what is Judged in Court.

For Court proposes, determining 'Justification' for such an extreme occurrence; killing another in Self-Defense, is extraordinarily complicated. Said justification is completely dependent upon how reasonable one's perception of impending death may be, combined with that persons' ability to adequately articulate its justification to a naysaying critic. As you'll soon learn, surviving a Deadly Encounter, is much more than defeating the person(s) trying to kill you. *ZuluShield* will help uncover the answers you've been looking for. It also provides you the easiest step-by-step process towards preparing yourself today so you can avoid a legal disaster tomorrow.

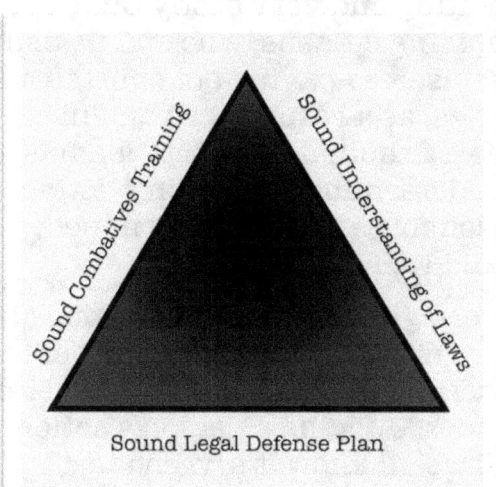

Sound Legal Defense Plan

In discussing the topic of Firearms Self-Defense, most people unintentionally focus on only one aspect, the 'Purchase' of a firearm. Unfortunately, the vast majority of armed citizens completely ignore three other equally important elements:

1. Without sound combatives training, your fancy new firearm is useless and in all reality places you and others at greater risk.

2. Without sound understanding of the laws associated with Self-Defense, there's no way for you to develop a decision making process which provides reasonable responses to perceived threats.

3. Without a sound Legal Defense plan, should you be forced to actually use Deadly Force in defense of your life or someone else's, your entire Legal Defense strategy will be based on 'Chance'.

The intent of this guide is to provide you with a comprehensive, step-by-step approach to the development of a bulletproof, Proactive Firearms Legal Defense.

In your lifetime, you're likely to spend hundreds if not thousands of dollars on firearms and accessories, all with the expectation; that if required, you'll have the capability of effectively defending your life, should someone try and take it. If, however, you take time and invest in the proactive approach which this guide offers, you'll be prepared for both the battle and the war. Should you actually find yourself at the focal point of a complicated Criminal and or a Civil legal proceeding, your diligence now will pay dividends tomorrow.

Generally speaking, when the average person thinks about the possibility of someday needing to defend their lives with a firearm, they stop short at assuming their actions will undoubtedly be found Justified. Their conclusion is that because they would have been confronted by someone who's not only breaking the law but also poses an actual threat to their lives, and assume that somehow the authorities will swoop in to prove their innocence. It all goes back to the superhero cartoons we grew-up on as kids, where the concept that 'Good' always prevails over 'Evil', was installed deep within our psyche. Frustratingly though, it really boils down to who's story makes the most sense, or how well that person is able to articulate the facts, which land on the side of 'Perceived Reason'.

Similarly, when the average person thinks about the aftermath of a Deadly Force Encounter; a circumstance where the required use of Deadly Physical Force is appropriate in the protection of 'Life', they stall, assuming that if law enforcement officers believe them, then it's a wrap. This too couldn't be more inaccurate. Most people fail to understand the gravity of such a circumstance. What they don't realize is just how badly things tend to snowball, directly follow such an incident. Even if Police find your actions reasonable, a Civil Court may likely come to a completely different conclusion.

Simply put, being found 'Criminally Justified' in the use of Deadly Force, doesn't automatically protect you from a devastating and very costly Civil Court battle, which can drag on for years. Many law abiding citizens; who end up using Criminally Justified Deadly Force, often find themselves paying-out substantial Civil penalties; to the offender's family of all things, as a result of 'Wrongful Death' lawsuits. This is even true in cases where a Criminal Investigation has been conducted and an actual District Attorney, determined a person's actions to have been completely and unequivocally reasonable and thus determined, Criminal charges were NOT warranted and should NOT be pursued.

What's true is that, 'The Law', is as much a foreign language as Klingon is to the average everyday person. The average armed citizen's understanding of the Judicial Process is general at best and is also horribly misguided and completely influenced by what they've seen on TV or in movies. Judging a person's actions on paper may appear to be simple. For instance, we all know it's wrong to murder, cheat and or steal. However, the waters quickly get murky when it relates to Self-Defense. The basic definition of murder is the unlawful Homicide of another. Killing someone in Self-Defense is also considered homicide.

Determining if a homicide is lawful either Criminally and or Civilly, is not necessarily a black and white issue and can often times be extremely gray.

This is the sad reality of our convoluted Justice System, where 'Good' doesn't always prevail. What's more, the vast majority of everyday, law abiding citizens, haven't the foggiest understanding of the Civil Justice System or how it directly relates to their use of Self-Defense. Unfortunate many otherwise innocent, people's lives and their families lives, are completely turned upside-down or even destroyed, due to their unintentional ignorance of the legal war they'll face directly following the use of Self-Defense, especially if it results in the death of another. As if to pour salt on a wound, the aftermath of these incidents typically spill over into the public domain, where the media circus takes you on the rollercoaster ride of your life. It's here, where media outlets turn your otherwise private life, into a public spectacle. Consider the 'Trayvon Martin' case for example. Just think about what George Zimmerman was faced with and what he had to endure. Regardless of your opinion of the incident, are you prepared for a legal battle of that magnitude? You need to be!

Equally frightening, is the complete lack of foresight the average armed citizen has to the unavoidable Criminal Investigation, which immediately follows EVERY use of Deadly Force. Don't mistake it, there is no maybe. If you use Deadly Force, there will be an extremely intrusive Criminal Investigation and you will be its focus. In fact, this investigation will most certainly begin within minutes of you being involved in a fight for your very existence. Think about it, minutes after you've just snatched your life back from the grimy grips of a murderous criminal, and while you're catching your breath and checking for holes, you're going to be scrutinized like never before. In most cases the incident will be investigated by some type of a dedicated Major Crimes Team, meaning you should expect to see dozens of uniformed police officers, investigators, evidence technicians and other officials, all converging on your location and setting up camp for a protracted period of time. It will be the most emotionally charged, overwhelming happening you've ever imagined.

As long as your actions are reasonably rational, authorities should eventually find you 'Criminally Justified.' That means no charges will be brought and the Criminal portion of the investigation will conclude. However, in more complicated Self-Defense cases where the facts, circumstances and evidence are more difficult to evaluate, investigators often choose to postpone potential arrests the day of such incidents. That doesn't mean it's over though. Even if they don't initially arrest you; if investigators don't make it clear that you're no longer under investigation, then you must assume you are and are likely being surveilled. These types of investigations are protracted at best. They can easily last months, years and in some cases are put on pause and labeled 'Unsolved', where investigators wait in hopes new evidence eventually surfaces. However, if all the evidence is gathered and a case is too difficult to determine either way, police will likely forward their findings to the District Attorney. It is the District Attorney who has the final say on determining if charges should be brought against you.

It's important to understand that no investigation is perfect. Unfortunately, there are times when Criminal charges are filed against completely innocent people. Sometimes those horribly sad cases result in an innocent person actually being sent to jail. This can occur because the initial investigation was conducted poorly by inexperienced investigators, or in cases where evidence may have been tampered with. However, typically it's because of a failure on the part of the victim who defended themselves. What this means it that during the initial police contact the person who acted in Self-Defense, failed to adequately articulate the reasonableness and extreme urgency for their actions.

In these types cases, an arrest is eventually made. If bail is authorized, bail amounts are typically no less than a few hundred thousand dollars. So, unless you can somehow acquire large sums of cash, you're likely to be stuck fighting your case from a jail cell, while waiting for the 'Wheels of Justice' to prove your innocence. A scenario like this where the Victim who acted in Self-Defense and who failed to properly articulate the facts during initial police contact, means their innocence will usually be proven because their attorney's will be able to present those facts in trial. However, this would only come to fruition after an extraordinarily lengthy process, requiring a substantial amount of monetary resource. Think about it, if you're left fighting your case from a jail cell, that means you're not working. No work means no income and no income, spells disaster for most families these days, since the typical family requires two solid incomes.

You must ask yourself, have you prepared for the possibility of fighting for your innocence from the confines of a jail cell? Do you even know where to begin with directing family members or friends on how to get in contact with your attorney? Do you already have an attorney whose familiar with Self-Defense claims? How about a list of back-up attorney's, who can be notified at a moment's notice? If you haven't thought hard about this and developed a strategy, you're like 99% of all the other law abiding, legally armed citizens, who are only one bad day away from their worst nightmare.

What people don't realize, is a District Attorney's only understanding of the incident in question, is completely isolated to the facts presented in a police officer's report. The accuracy of such a report is totally dependent upon the evidence found during the investigation and how well you and possible witnesses articulated the facts, so as to support both your actions and the evidence. On top of this, most people don't understand the gravity of such an investigation. Truth is, should you use Deadly Force, a police investigation will be focused on determining if you committed or attempted to commit Murder, it's intent is not on proving your innocence.

The concept of 'Innocent Until Proven Guilty' is completely misunderstood and for the most part a complete misnomer. From the perspective of a seasoned Criminal Investigator, the reality is that a police officer investigating such an incident, believes everybody is 'Guilty' until they prove themselves innocent. While that may not be Politically Correct, its just human nature. That doesn't mean they round everyone up and whisk them off to jail. What it means is that unfortunately they will inevitably form biases and preconceived perspectives of a person's guilt or innocence. It's these unavoidable, human biases, which can easily cause even a seasoned investigator to misread circumstances and inadvertently misrepresent facts and evidence to your detriment. Again it's just human nature. This is how innocent people end up being arrested and convicted of crimes they never committed.

Most armed citizens have never properly thought through this reality. They don't realize this until they're face to face with Detective Sipowicz, who's firing-off strategically orchestrated questions for hours on end with no relent. They also fail to understand they'll be thrust into this whirlwind, directly following the most stressful incident they've likely ever encountered. The stress of such an incident directly affects one's ability to even comprehend this form of questioning, let alone be able to effectively and accurately articulate their innocence. If that's not bad enough, they've also never connected the dots to realize, that should they be found guilty of murder, the consequences are inevitably, life imprisonment or in some cases, death.

Physical confrontations with firearms; and even unarmed physical conflict, are the most fluidly dynamic environments one could ever find themselves. It's the most chaotically charged, out of control, consistently changing set of circumstances, which is measured in splits of seconds and whose force is greater than the convergence of entire oceans. In fact, the overwhelming and unavoidable tidal wave of physiological and psychological effects during such an incident, rates up there with an apocalyptic tsunami. Armed confrontations aren't action movies or video games. There's no do-overs or re-spawning and your errors are immediately accompanied by devastatingly lethal consequences.

Because of this, things don't always pan-out how one would expect. It's not always cut and dry. It's not always going to appear that you're actually the Victim of a deadly attack. For an example you could be faced with a scenario where you are confronted by an unarmed suspect; who at the time and under the circumstances is an obvious risk to your very existence. Yet the evidence found during an investigation, might not be so clear. It's entirely possible it may appear to police that you executed or unlawfully shot an unarmed person, resulting in their untimely death. It's also completely probable, that such a situation could appear, that you did so by shooting an unarmed victim in the back and the only proof of your innocence is your testimony.

How you say? It all boils down to Action vs. Reaction. Basically the time it takes you to react to the aggressor, formulate your Defensive Response and finally shoot said aggressor, during the lag-time or your response and as your placing your finger on the trigger, the aggressor could have moved or even turned their back. Or the aggressor falls to the ground sideways, while you're actively shooting them. Once you've made the decision to shoot, it takes a substantial amount of time to stop shooting, especially during sensory overload. It's completely feasible that it could take you two-seconds for your brain to realize the bad guy's no longer a 'Threat' and communicate that to your finger that's still squeezing the trigger as fast as it can.

These types of scenarios are actually very common during police shootings and leave the public assuming officers executed unarmed persons, when in actual fact they had not. It should be noted that even under such daunting circumstances, police officers involved in shootings have unions and a whole host of legal resources backing them in their corner and on standby at all times. These resources are readily capable of assisting in their Legal Defense. The average citizen simply doesn't have this. All they have is their word and their bond and an extremely limited amount of monetary resource.

You need a plan ahead of time. Your plan should be a proactive approach to tomorrow's legal battle. This proactive approach should be capable of defending your innocence, even under the most difficulty impossible circumstances. It's critical that this Defense Strategy be well orchestrated and capable of providing countless examples for why your actions aren't only justified, but are so bulletproof, that they actually keep you out of the whirlwind of Civil proceedings altogether. This guide is completely capable of assisting in your development of just that, a bulletproof Firearms Legal Defense. Should you end up in the midst of such proceedings, *ZuluShield* will be more valuable to you than you could ever imagine.

Chapter 1

Not Guilty!

Not Guilty! Now of course, if for any reason you find yourself in Court following the use of Self-Defense, these are the words you fully expect to hear. However, achieving such a windfall during a Self-Defense case, is an extremely difficult task. That's because incidents involving Self-Defense are typically the most difficult cases to prove, especially when the circumstances are murky or when the suspect is unarmed. Even in instances where a Defendant is completely Innocent, if they find themselves in Criminal Court, it means the police and the District Attorney believe they've either committed murdered, attempted to murder someone or at best unlawfully caused harm to another. You can more than guarantee the authorities will do everything within their power to prove their case. So what's your plan?

I'm sure you've heard the saying "It's better to be judged by twelve than carried by six." On one hand, there is obvious truth to the fact that the number-one priority, when faced with a Deadly Threat to your existence, is to survive the battle and breathe another day. However, an objective valuation of this concept doesn't mean being judged by six is a good thing, it simply means you're still breathing. Unfortunately, if you wind-up being the focus of a Capital Murder or say even a Negligent Homicide proceeding, you're likely to feel that 'Breathing' isn't exactly a gift. Most people haven't a clue as to just how devastatingly, life altering, both Criminal and Civil battles actually are. Even if you win, you are in for an equally stressful struggle to that which got you into the situation in the first place.

Having such a cavalier, narrow-minded approach to Self-Defense may actually cost you much, much more than you're prepared or even capable of affording. This type of perspective is far too passive. It greatly limits your Legal Defense potential, forcing you to sit-by today, while you 'Wait', all the while expecting that when you eventually come face-to-face with a Deadly Threat, you'll determine what to do then. Basically you set yourself up for a kneejerk reaction. Are you willing to bet your life on a crapshoot like that, or would rather put some effort into finding the BEST Legal Defense Strategy today for tomorrow's legal battle?

What if I told you there was a way to have your cake and eat it too, survive the encounter and avoid a lengthy Court battle, absent the need of being judged altogether? The world renowned tactical strategist Sun Tzu warns us to "know" our enemy and to "fight" our battle a thousand times before even meeting our adversary. The theory he proposes is obvious. In order to assure victory; beyond mere survival, in order to dominate the field-of-battle, one must first and foremost prepare mentally. Sun Tzu's suggestion is to become the 'Master' of strategy rather than be made a 'Slave' or be made subject to the 'Act' of war. His thesis suggests that victory through conflict has much less to do with the 'Kinesis' of battle, than it does with the practiced cognitive composition of its planning.

Waiting to hear a Judge proclaim, "Not Guilty!" as they slam their gavel to the table during a Negligent Homicide or Wrongful Death proceeding, is an extraordinarily expensive way to win. No matter how right you are or how justified you assume your actions may have been, if you end-up on the opposing side of the table to a Criminal or Civil Law Judge, you should expect your legal fees to easily exceed a hundred thousand dollars or more and that's only if you win. Are you prepared to take out a second mortgage today? If you're like the vast majority of cash strapped, hard working, everyday citizens just struggling to survive, then you'd agree, you would have a better chance at hitting the Powerball than you would at landing a loan like this. If you're one of the fortunate; more financially sound few, just because you can afford a good attorney, doesn't mean you're any better off. In actual fact, your liability exposure Criminally is equal to that of a less financially-set individual, but your exposure Civilly is exponentially greater. If you appear to have loads of cash, you better expect you're a huge target and will be making a multi-million-dollar settlement at best, unless you protect yourself today.

As opposed to settling for a Passive Defense, why not opt for a Proactive Approach that preemptively establishes strategic buffers and insulates you against legal action altogether? That's exactly what this manual is designed to do. However, this can only occur if you take the adequate steps and invest real time and effort today and adhere to its practice. This chapter focuses on the bedrock of such a defense and should be studied very, very closely. In fact, it's highly suggested you read this chapter at least twice prior to proceeding.

Initiating a Proactive Defense:

Most legally armed citizens simply aren't prepared for the devastating and life altering Criminal and or Civil penalties associated with the use of Self-Defense. It's a subject almost completely overlooked by most firearms and concealed-carry instructors all-together. While they may touch on the laws associated with Self-Defense and they may even mention the possibilities of Prosecution, nobody offers any real solutions should that possibility become reality. Instead they focus on the obvious, the mastering of your firearm. Don't get me wrong, investing in quality firearms training is essential and should be compulsory and a priority in anyone's thought process. However, even the most highly trained tactical professional could easily find themselves on the receiving end of a most disastrous Criminal and or Civil battle.

I'm sure you've also heard, "the best defense is a good offense." This couldn't be truer, especially when it relates to defending one's actions after the use of Self-Defense. What you do today, makes all the difference tomorrow. Being proactive, by calculating and then developing the MOST effective Legal Defense, is just as important as being able to accurately press the trigger tomorrow. On top of this, the byproduct of Forward Thought is 'Continual' and affords you with a smorgasbord of Self-Defense Response options options for any given problem. What this means is by taking the time today to prepare your Legal Defense, you will inevitably be forced to contemplate possible scenarios which may require a Self-Defense Response. This contemplation requires active-thought. In turn you end up with multiply ways to address a particular type of threat, where each option is based on Reason, is perpetually intelligent, astute and minimizes poor judgment errors. Forward-thinking protects you both legally and physically. That's the genius behind the *ZuluShield* approach, is the difference between playing Chess rather than being stuck playing Checkers.

Is it really that bad?

Self-Defense claims are among the most 'Subjective' you'll ever find. For the most part your Defense is founded on your perspective or on a 'Thought.' It's the intangibility of this Thought, which adds a fair amount of difficulty when it comes to articulating one's justification for a particular set of actions. Later on, when you're preparing for Court, your attorney tries to find ways to first, grasp the totality of the perspective you had at the time of the incident, balance that with the peripheral circumstances surrounding that incident; to better understand why you did what you did, then finally find a way to make the reasonableness of your actions more tangible, by giving it contextual structure so it can be easily seen, understood and felt in the hearts and minds of the Judge and or Jury.

To a third-party looking in after the fact; like a Judge or Jury member, your actions back on the day of the incident, may appear to have been completely hypothetically based and be easily misunderstood as an overreaction to an unreasonable assumption of impending danger. Your Defense for said actions is completely reliant on your individual ability to verbally describe the 'Totality-of-the-Circumstances' at the very moment of that incident and clearly show exactly why you chose the course of action you did and then support all that with hard facts. You need to find a way to turn the hypothetical into a 'Premonition of Fact'. You do that by clearly articulating the totality of the situation you faced and mirror those circumstances with real-world examples of similar incidents which required other people to choose a similar type of response to a Deadly Threat.

Before you can do this, you must first understand the concept of Totality-of-the-Circumstances. This is a complete rundown of EVERTHING related to the incident in question. This includes, persons present, hazards; whether obvious or perceived, health related factors, past experiences or training, topography and layout of your immediate environment, what was said and or done before ad during the incident and the list goes on and on. This should send shivers up and down your spine. You see the vast majority of people are not well-spoken, they're not eloquent, nor do they express themselves in a manner of intellect or clarity. In fact, most people's vocabulary consists of watered down jargon, derived from a glossary of vernacular slang and generalizations.

It's not in our habits as everyday people, to communicate with much clarity at all. Yet in Court, the accuracy of your testimony needs to be as focused as a laser's beam. For example, the average everyday person typically speaks in paraphrases. For instance, when describing someone with tons of money, a person may say, they have "deep pockets." For the most part, this would be understood, but in Court this could be misunderstood to mean a person literally has Deep Pockets. This also leaves a question as to which pockets, their pant's, their jacket or both? As another example someone could say, they were lying on the beach "catching some rays." Again, most people would understand this to mean that person was sunbathing at the beach. However, for Court purposes this could also mean an individual laid down on a beach and was literally fishing for stingrays. My point is, your entire proof of innocence balances on your ability to communicate exactly what occurred and why it occurred, with such clarity that everyone fully understands what you've said without the slightest chance of misunderstanding. You must also do this under the daunting stresses of Court itself and you most certainly wouldn't have slept for days leading up to such testimony. On top of all this, your testimony in Court must also be consistent with any other statements or bits of information you've volunteered during the investigation, meaning any inconsistencies could easily give the appearance of untruthfulness.

In many other types of cases, determining Right from Wrong is a much easier task. For instance, if you're caught shoplifting a bag of potato chips from a local 7-11, the case is much more 'Objective' by nature. In this case the Prosecution will likely use videotape evidence of you physically removing the bag of chips from the shelf and then stuffing them in your pocket. Next, the video shows you sneaking out of the store without paying. Cases like these are pretty cut and dry, unless you can muster up a reasonable excuse that you somehow 'Forgot' to pay, you're guilty because there's no other logical reason why you'd stuff the chips in your pants and walk out.

However, determining whether someone's 'Perspective' of impending mortal danger is reasonable or not, isn't so easily attained. This is especially true if the aggressor was unarmed at the time of attack. Let's say you're in a sports bar and are confronted. Video tape evidence in this case could show the aggressor confronting you. It could also show that all you were doing was minding your own business while you visited with friends. The video could even show what appears to be a verbal back and forth argument between the two of you with lots of hand gestures. Next, it could show the aggressor taking a step towards you and lastly as though he was about to turn the altercation into a physical one, the video evidence would then show you pulling a firearm and shooting the otherwise unarmed patron. Now what? How do you explain your actions away as being Reasonable?

What the video will likely NOT show, is the aggressor telling you he was an MMA fighter, while making repeated threats of bodily harm. In this case, the video evidence will not show how this information impacted your psyche and why it made the bells and whistles go off in your head. The video evidence won't show how you connected the dots and determined that, although he was not armed, the fact that you believed he was an MMA fighter, lead you to believe that he was very well trained in the art of hand-to-hand combatives and could easily inflict serious bodily harm or even cause your untimely death. The video evidence also won't show your assumption that because he's in a bar and possibly intoxicated, he posses even greater risk to your safety, since his lack of faculties could have reasonably compromised his thought process, to the point that he could get so enraged, that he may not stop beating you and would have to be pulled off of you. On top of all this, the video evidence will not show your belief or your 'Intangible Thought' that even one punch from an individual like this, could actually cause your death. It would also not communicate that the basis by which the totality of your assumptions are founded, pertain to a number of things you've learned in the past relating to physical confrontation and the associated risks to your physical wellbeing. This is where effective articulation makes all the difference because without it, you just killed an unarmed man on video, in cold-blood.

Of course the obvious culprit for ending up in Court after the use of a firearm for Self-Defense, usually means you've fired your weapon and killed or gravely injured another person in the process. But what about Menacing? This is when you draw and point your firearm at another and you don't actually fire your weapon. Instead, you simply point it at them, there by communicating your intent to use it should they continue to be a 'Threat'.

Obviously pointing a firearm at someone is in and of itself a Threat and would reasonably leave the other person to assume you'll act on that threat and fire. What if that's all you do and the bad guy backs down? Now the police are called and somehow you're accused of being the aggressor since the other guy was unarmed and didn't even attack you? If you can't articulate a reasonable explanation for why your actions were warranted, then you're in for an extremely painful lesson. Is there such a thing as 'Justified Menacing'. Is there a basis by which it becomes reasonable to brandish a firearm and point it at another, before things have actually escalated to the point that you finally need to shoot? Have you considered how you would defend against this type of Self-Defense claim? Losing this argument in Court, means you'd be convicted of a very serious felony with a deadly weapon and would not only see real jail time, but you'd also lose your Second Amendment Right altogether.

What if I told you that Science can win this battle for you and that the scientific theory of 'Action vs. Reaction' will easily show why it's completely reasonable to brandish your firearm long before you're justified to actually shoot? What if I also told you there are many studies to back this up and that one in particular; 'The 21-Foot Rule' or the 'Tueller Drill' can show just how unreasonable it would be to expect someone to wait for an aggressor to attack before brandishing much less firing their weapon in Self-Defense? How about the argument of Overkill? In terms of the Courts, 'Overkill' is when someone claims to have shot another in Self-Defense, yet evidence shows they actually emptied their firearm's magazine and shot the assailant fifteen or sixteen times and unless justified, is seen as being 'Cruel and Unreasonable'. How in the world could this be reasonable? How could you defend such actions?

This is where educating yourself on the scientific dynamics of Deadly Force Encounters comes into play and why it makes all the difference in Court. There are many scientifically proven factors associated with armed conflict, which directly effects how one responds under such stress. One of those areas pertains to the lag –time associated with decision making, while under extreme amounts of Combat Stress. A Court's judgment process is completely based on Reason. If you can present a reasonable explanation for why you did what you did; be it brandish your firearm ahead of time or continued to fire even after the Threat falls to the ground, then the issues of Overkill and or Menacing are easily overcome.

The study of this science is commonly referred to as 'Force Science' and is a hugely important source of data you should immerse yourself in today. As you'll soon learn, the sheer 'Gravity' of this type of data can make all the difference and it's something your attorney WON'T think of. That's precisely why this manual was designed. It gives you the ability to gather data they won't think of, ahead of time and then organize and communicate this vital information and translate that data in a way that's palatable to your attorney. The topic of Force Science will be covered in much more detail later on in Chapter (3).

So what does 'The Law' say?

As I've mentioned previously, there are no hard fast, black and white rules pertaining to Self-Defense. Self-Defense laws are extremely broad and the basis by which they're weighed, is completely depended upon the 'Perceived Actions' of another and how those assumed actions threaten another's wellbeing. For instance, if you're sitting quietly in your seat at a movie theater and someone walks up and punches you in the face, you may or may not be justified in shooting them. It depends on the Totality-of-the-Circumstances.

Or in other words:

1. Did you sustain injury?

2. Are you light headed, dazed or on the verge of losing consciousness?

3. Is the aggressor still an Active Threat even after the initial punch?

4. Could the aggressor's next punch cause life-threatening injury?

5. Are you trapped or confined leaving you with no reasonable way to flee?

6. Are you in fear for your life or someone else's?

These are only a few extremely important factors which help determine justification. If the answer is a resounding YES!!! to these questions, then you MIGHT be justified in the use of a firearm against an otherwise unarmed attacker. Notice I said 'Might'. Under different circumstances however, Deadly Force may NOT be justified.

These are precisely the kinds of questions presented to a 72 year-old retired cop who shot and killed an unarmed man during an altercation at a movie theater in Florida. He was arrested and charged with Second Degree Murder. His bail was set at a whopping $150,000. This meant unless he could somehow come up with hard cash, he would fight for his innocence behind bars until his trial concluded. As of the writing of this book, nearly two years have passed since this incident and his trial has still not been set. Could you come up with $150,000 today? Can you imagine the continued cost beyond this just to defend your innocence much less the stress you'd be enduring while waiting for trial? Keep in mind, a trial like this, with over twenty-two witnesses, could drag on for months, so it's completely feasible that this man won't learn his fate for another year. This; my friend, is only the Criminal aspect. When it comes to Civil

Liability, I can guarantee the family of the man killed, will most certainly bring a Wrongful Death suit against him and by the looks of it, he's in for a whole other world of SUCK.

So when attempting to decode 'The Law' don't expect it to give you a definitive justified action for a particular set of circumstances. It's also very important to understand that there are a multitude of State and Federal laws, which directly relate to weapons, conduct and Self-Defense. There are also many Municipal and County codes and ordnances, which also come into play. All of these will play a pivotal role in determining whether your actions are truly justified or not.

To better understand a few VERY important concepts, let's explore some basic legal definitions pertaining to Use of Force. Keep in mind it is essential that you refer to your particular Stat's actual legal definitions as they may differ slightly from State to State. Most States provide a hyperlink to their Criminal Codes and their definitions on their webpage. Get familiar with it and download your States statutes pertaining to Self-Defense. Retain this information and file it away in your *ZuluShield Archive*.

Justified Physical Force...

"A private citizen is justified in using Physical Force for Self-Defense or the defense of a third party, from what the person reasonably believes to be the use or imminent use of unlawful Physical Force. This person is justified in using the degree of Physical Force which that person reasonably believes to be necessary for the purpose of stopping the other person's unlawful actions."

Deadly Physical Force

"Physical Force that under the circumstances in which it is used, is readily capable of causing serious physical injury."

Justified Deadly Physical Force

"A private citizen is justified in using Deadly Physical Force for Self-Defense or the defense of a third party if that person reasonably believes another person is using or about to use Unlawful Deadly Physical Force."

Serious Physical Injury

"Physical injury which creates a substantial risk of death."

Reasonable

"Agreeable to sound judgment and logic, does not exceed the limits of prescribed reason, is rational and is not excessive."

Clear as mud?

Did you notice how vague these definitions actually are? For instance, the justified use of both Physical and Deadly Force are completely based on the word 'Reasonable'. It couldn't get more ambiguous than that. Reasonableness is what I call a 'Lukewarm Word'. It's neither here nor there, up or down, left or right. Yet, it's the foundation of our entire Judicial System. The scale which Lady Justice holds in her hands, is a symbol of this concept. It speaks to the balance of reason. Is said action or perception of that action, feasible, plausible, prudent, rational and or sensible? This is where the importance of philosophical articulation comes into play. Reasonableness is derived from your ability to describe the Totality-of-the-Circumstances including what you saw, assumed and why you did what you did, in a manner that's palatable to the naysayer. To win, her scale must balance.

Similarly, Deadly Physical Force and Serious Physical Injury are also based on ambiguity. The concepts of 'Readily Capable' and 'Substantial Risk' are both subject to opinion and perspective. One could easily argue that a punch to the face does NOT justify the use of Deadly Physical Force. However, if for instance you articulate the fact that the offender appeared to be much larger than you and that his punch left you in a daze. If you also articulated that you were in a vulnerable position with no way out and that the offender was able to use all his weight with each of his punches; since he was standing above, you. If you believed it likely and feared that he would continue his course of action, then one could easily argue why Deadly Physical Force is justified, even if the offender is completely unarmed.

To sum things up, Justified Use of Force is a balanced perspective of how you view something and if your point-of-view is sensible to another reasonable person. If it is, then your Use of Force was justified. The amount and type of Physical Force is also a balance of objective view points. If you are defending against something that could actually kill you, then you can use Deadly Physical Force in return. However, if another person's actions would not likely cause death, then you're limited and ONLY justified in using the amount of Physical Force which is necessary and capable of bringing a stop to the attack or control over your aggressor.

Protecting property...

So you're returning from the store and see someone attempting to steal your car. Do you shoot? Or you arrive home and catch a Burglar in the act as they're exiting the back door of your home, with your brand new $3,000 flat screen TV. Do you shoot? While some states do authorize the use of Deadly Physical Force in protecting physical property, it is _HIGHLY_ recommended that you do _NOT_ use Deadly Physical Force in these situations. While you may be Criminally Justified, it's almost guaranteed you will be hit with a very expensive Wrongful Death Civil suit. Ask yourself; is the property you're attempting to protect worth $2-$3 million, plus attorney's fees?

Now let's say you're returning to your car and witness someone breaking into it, only this time your kids are in the backseat. Or you arrive home to witness someone kicking the door into your house and your family waits inside.

Under these circumstances the 'Intent' for why you would choose to use Deadly Physical Force is different because now your intent is to protect 'Life' not property. The use of Deadly Physical Force to prevent Home Invasions and Kidnappings are almost always justified, as long as you're able to effectively accurately articulate the Totality-of-the-Circumstances.

Robberies...

Robberies and burglaries are often misunderstood. A robbery occurs when someone attempts to unlawfully take something of value from another, through the use or threatened use of Physical Force. As mentioned above it is NOT advisable to use Deadly Physical Force to protect your property even if the robber is trying to steal your wallet with $1,000 cash in it. However, robberies automatically introduce one extremely dangerous byproduct. The aggressor IS either using or threatening to use Physical Force and IS typically armed or is giving the impression that they are armed. If you reasonably believe and fear that the threatened Physical Force could actually kill you, then their threated force would give you a reasonable basis for using Deadly Physical Force in return. In this case you're protecting your Life not your property. It's this slight shift of 'Intangible Thought' which makes all the difference. Being proactive and thinking through things today, gives you the ability to present an intellectual basis for your actions tomorrow.

Burglaries...

A burglary occurs when someone unlawfully enters a primes or dwelling with the intent to commit a crime. Typically, a burglar's intent is to steal property similar to that of a robber stealing your wallet. However, now days there's been a recent explosion of Home Invasion Robberies, where the offender's intent is much more than the theft of property.

A quick Google search for 'Home Invasion Robberies' will easily give you hundreds of examples of why it's completely reasonable to use Deadly Physical Force to protect against a Home Invasion. But how do you know the assailant's intent is to commit a violent act or just theft? You don't until it's too late. That's where this manual can make all the difference. It provides you an extremely well organized means of retaining actual real-world occurrences, which easily support one's decision to use Deadly Physical Force under those circumstances. The downloading of articles, images and even videos of real-world Home Invasions and other types of Robberies are the kinds of evidence which speak for themselves and can make all the difference in your future Legal Defense. These are the Chess pieces of success you play today, which will quickly and vividly prove the justification of your actions tomorrow.

Being able to present to a Judge and or Jury, an image of the physical injuries sustained by a victim of a Home Invasion Robbery, will stick with that person all the way thorough your trial. Having the ability to reference the random 2007 Cheshire, Connecticut Home Invasion of a family, where a father, his wife and their 11 and 17 year old daughters were beat with baseball bats and bound, where the wife was forced to withdraw $15,000 from her bank and if it couldn't have been worse, the assailants continually beat, raped and tortured the wife and daughters in front of the father over a seven hour period, then torched the house leaving them all to die, this is what compels a third-party to not only see but also feel the degree of fear and anguish that would reasonably lead you to using Deadly Physical Force. In this case the father randomly freed himself but has to live the rest of his days with the vivid memory of his dying wife and kids whom he was hapless to save.

If you are confronted at home, there's no way to know what to expect. In the Cheshire incident, the wife had been dropped off at her bank by one of the suspects. She actually reported the incident to staff who notified police. She described the suspects by their appearance but added that the suspects at this point were "being nice" and suggested she believed they just wanted money. Sadly, the wife exited the bank with the cash and met up with her would be killer before police could arrive.

Think about it, you're typically at your lowest level of awareness when you're at your home. If your door is kicked-in, you usually won't even have adequate time to safely flee, and you're likely accompanied by your family who are also all in immediate danger. Calling 911 only notifies the police that you have a problem. In the Cheshire incident, bank staff notified police who in turn set-up surveillance around the residence, all while this poor family was being raped, tortured and murdered.

Attempting to negotiate, plead for your life, or even trying to go along with the assailant's demands, has time and time again proven NOT to turn out well. But why do authorities advise people to do so, because police don't like vigilantism and all feel that by encouraging potential victims to 'Fight' could bring undue liability on the agency should that person be killed or injured, fighting. It's up to you to determine how to solve that problem until help arrives. Complying with their wishes may work, or it may just seal your fate. If you believe there is a reasonable risk to your life or the lives of your family and you fear that death will result, then it's completely reasonable for you to use Deadly Physical Force to protect said Life. Remember it's about protecting life <u>NOT</u> property.

Shooting Kill...

Here's a subject that's rife with a multitude of contradicting positions of opinion. First of all, shooting to 'Wound' or injure, is complete nonsense and totally unreasonable and impractical. It can actually increase your chances of collateral damage, causing you to wound or even kill an innocent third-party, thereby exponentially exposing you to unneeded Criminal and Civil liability. It's hard enough to shoot a moving human torso, which is on average about 16-20" by 24", let alone trying to shoot someone's leg, which is moving and is say 6" wide or their arm which is 3" wide. Shooting to wound is for the movies, it's NOT a safe bet for a winning Legal Defense.

The concept of 'Shooting to Kill' is a bit more complicated these days. Instead, the more Politically Correct term would be to 'Shoot to Stop the Threat'. This couldn't be a more ambiguous non-answer if you tried. One thing I've never understood is why people are so afraid to say that their intent is to 'Kill' a person who's trying to 'murder' them? Think about it, if you are faced with a scenario where a person poses a reasonable threat to your very existence, and your decision is to use 'Deadly' Physical Force, then why is it so wrong to say that upon making such an extreme decision, your intent was to KILL the Threat before they killed you or someone else?

The true reason for this confusion is what I refer to as the 'Pussification of America'. While I'll admit this term could easily offend some, I insist that learning to harness 'Offense' is exactly what's missing. We have become so ultra politically correct that we can't call black, 'Black', white, 'White', Christmas, 'Christmas' or even encourage our children to pledge allegiance to our Flag at school. We are so afraid to offend or say something that might cause another discomfort, that we 'The People' have for a long time now, censored ourselves. Sure its politer to be tactful with our vernacular, however failing to instruct people to KILL their Threat, while at the same time encouraging them to use 'DEADLY' Physical Force, is insanity. Doing so only causes confusion on the part of the person whose life is in the balance. If we aren't at liberty to define Right from Wrong and call things what they are, then we don't have Liberty at all.

If you don't know how to live and breathe 'Through' offense, then how in the world do you expect to survive an out-of-control deadly attack, which is the most offensively lethal reality you'll ever know? A tank earns its resilience to defeat and in so it's supremacy on the battle field by being 'Thick-skinned'. This essential quality is precisely what's missing in our society today and why so many people allow themselves to be victimized as apposed to being prepared and ready to defend their lives despite offense.

Don't be afraid to be clear and concise with your intentions in Court. If you're justified to use Deadly Physical Force, then you are justified in <u>KILLING</u> another in Self-Defense. The concept of 'Shooting to Stop the Threat' may sound all prim and proper, but it actually leaves an open door to a whole host of problems. How? If you testify that your intent was not to kill but rather to 'Stop' the Threat, then you're basically saying that you believed at the time that you were justified in simply 'Stopping' the Threat, not 'Killing' them. Now if circumstances were such that the Prosecution and or Plaintiff were able to argue that the Threat had ceased to be a 'Threat' long before you stopped shooting, then the concept of 'Overkill' becomes a hurdle you must overcome. While we've already discussed some ways of overcoming this issue, avoiding this argument altogether by simply being clear and concise, is by far a less complicated approach. Don't be afraid to be truthful. As long as you can present a reasonable reason why your use of DEADLY Physical Force was justified, then the Courts have already determined your justification in <u>KILLING</u> your Threat.

Warning Shots...

Here again we are faced with yet another topic rampant with tons of misguided points of view. The intent of this manual is to provide you with the best avenue for a winning Legal Defense. For that reason, I strongly suggest that you do <u>NOT</u> fire Warning Shots. Even if your State has a law in place, which allows for such a circumstance. Firing Warning Shots actually works against you in every way.

It goes without saying that firearms are extremely dangerous tools of survival and should be used with utmost safety. Discharging a firearm under any circumstance automatically exposes you and others to extreme risk of injury and or death. Because of this, discharging a firearm also exposes the shooter to extreme Criminal and Civil Liability.

Bullets travel at thousands of feet-per-second. Intentionally firing a round into the ground next to you is foolish. Why, because that round is completely capable of ricocheting and poses the actual potential of hitting an innocent bystander, blocks or even a mile away. Firing into the air is even more dangerous. Since bullets have the ability to fly for over a mile and as physics tells us, "what goes up, must come down" that bullet is going to land somewhere and you are completely responsible for where and what that bullet lands on.

Think about it, innocent people die every day from gang style drive-by-shootings due to the gangbanger's inaccuracy by missing their intended target. Those misses either immediately hit unintended victims or ricochet and still have the potential to injure and or kill. Intentionally firing warning shots is no different than intentionally shooting to 'Miss' and if that miss hits the wrong person, then you are 100% liable and you WILL pay the consequences. Even *ZuluShield* would be of little to no help if you intentionally shoot to 'Miss'.

The truth about 'Fear'...

The concept of 'Fear' is an integral component of any Self-Defense Response. It's as unavoidable as the Sun is hot and when you're confronted with a Deadly Encounter, it WILL play a pivotal role in your decision making process. In our masculine macho society, Fear is a phenomenon we're taught to avoid at all costs as though it were The Plague. However, when it relates to one's decision to use Deadly Physical Force in Self-Defense, admitting your Fear must <u>NEVER</u> be avoided and or watered down. One of the most important ingredients to articulate about exactly 'Why' you chose to defend yourself, comes down to the 'Degree' of fear you actually experienced. Your entire Legal Defense rides on your ability to give Fear a number, to define its mass and effectively articulate its density. In order for your actions to be considered justified, you MUST articulate that the Assailant's actions caused you to FEAR for yours or a third-parties life. Without this admission, your hopes of being cleared go out the window. You must NEVER be shy to admit your level of fear when articulating the effects of the Assailant's actions on you. You didn't "worry" that you "could" be hurt, you FEARED that your life WOULD be taken and that 'Fear' was such that you had no other alternative, but to defend yourself. This is how honest and how clear you must be. The topic of Fear is covered in much more detail later in Chapter (3), where you'll learn the effects of this phenomenon and learn how to harness and tame it.

Criminal vs. Civil Court...

Our Justice System is comprised of two arms, the 'Criminal' and the 'Civil' arms of Justice. While there are some similarities in both, each has their own completely different set of standards and outcomes.

Most people are familiar with the Criminal arm. It's the 'Perry Mason' we grew up watching on TV. While it's entirely possible that you could be arrested even though you're completely innocent, the 'Burden of Proof' for a Criminal conviction is extremely high and referred to as being 'Beyond a Reasonable

Doubt.' This basically means the Prosecution must prove that there is 99.9% probability of your guilt and there isn't any rational or logical legally justified reason for why you did what you did. Remember the 'OJ Defense' where OJ Simpson made it appear in Court that his hand did not fit in the glove, which the Prosecution claimed the killer used during the act of murder? Well it worked and the saying stuck, "If it don't fit, you must acquit." All he had to do was present just ONE single form of Reasonable Doubt and he was acquitted of all charges.

Presenting Reasonable Doubt, while also defending against other more damaging concepts of guilt, is not an easy task. In fact, the 'OJ Defense' was a last ditch effort, accompanied by a few other examples of how the Prosecution's case had a few holes. If your Legal Defense strategy is limited to scavenging the Prosecution's evidence, for that single reasonably doubtful element of contradiction, then you have what's called a 'Reactionary Defense'. What I mean by this, is if you haven't already prepared and designed a 'Proactive Legal Defense' such as the one you'll develop with *ZuluShield*, then you're left with a knee-jerk reactionary Defense and are completely limited in your ability to counter a Prosecution's well strategized attack. Basically, you're left 'Waiting' and are stuck playing a game of Poker, hoping that you'll be able to guess the Prosecution's hand and catch them bluffing. But what if they don't bluff, what's your Defense against a solid offence? Utilizing the methods presented in this manual, makes the task of designing the most formidable Defense possible, as easy as 1, 2, 3. It will provide your attorney with a plethora of ready-to-use examples of very strategic Reasonable Doubt solutions, to counter even the most cunning offensive. This way you're not stuck waiting to see if say the Prosecutor's 'Glove' fits or not, like OJ.

The Civil arm of Justice is actually the one which is most likely to ruin you. It's also the one which the vast majority of armed citizens completely misunderstand or even overlook all together. Since It's the comical 'Judge Judy' type proceedings, we view these cases as trivial or some sort of act of comedy. Yet when it comes to a Deadly Force case, a Civil Courtroom is the very last place you'll ever want to find yourself.

You must always remember that just because you've been cleared Criminally, doesn't necessarily mean your legal battle is over. In fact, in any Self-Defense claim; where someone's been seriously injured or killed, if you don't prepare your Defense today, it's not a matter of 'If' you'll be sued but WHEN and how much it's going to cost you. That is unless you properly insulate yourself today. Even if you're found guilty and serving time Criminally, you can still be sued. Talk about a nightmare. The sad reality is that it's not uncommon for everyday, legally armed, law abiding citizens to end up in serious trouble Criminally, following the use of Self-Defense. It's also not uncommon for someone to not only lose their home but also end up owing millions of dollars in Civil penalties, even when that use of Self-Defense was found to be 100% justified by both the Police and District Attorneys.

A number of years ago, I learned of a very interesting case of justified Self-Defense and how it turned into a poor victim's nightmare Civilly. The just of the case was that a neurosurgeon started a fight in a bar resulting in the doctor's arrest. The surgeon; who was found to be the 'Aggressor' and eventually found guilty of the assault, successfully sued the victim in Civil Court. During the process of defending themselves, the victim and broke the surgeon's hand resulting in the surgeon being left legally disabled and unable to continue working as a neurosurgeon. Disgustingly, a Civil Court found the victim completely liable and penalized the victim in the sum of $1.5-million.

We hear about these cases all the time and still most people don't think it could ever happen to them. That is until they find themselves in the midst of their very Civil nightmare. The reality is that, if it can happen to 'Them' it can most definitely happen to you. Its up to YOU to protect against it.

The biggest difference between the two arms of Justice and your greatest threat during any Civil trial, is the Civil System's extremely low Burden of Proof. Civilly, all the Plaintiff has to show is that you 'More Likely Than Not' or by 'Preponderance of The Evidence' violated Civil Law. This is most closely related to a police officer's 'Probably Cause' to arrest. It's an extraordinarily low level of proof, amounting to only 50.01%. Basically, it's just a tip of the scale. During a Wrongful Death suit, such a low burden often proves to be insurmountable. The reason for this is how easy it is for the Plaintiff to bombard the Court with reason after reason for why their loved one should NOT have been killed. Often times all they have to do is come up with just one reasonably sounding argument that their loved one didn't actually pose a serious threat or that you could have just walked away.

Not only is the Burden of Proof extremely low during Civil proceedings, but in many cases the 'Burden' sits on the shoulders of the defendant, which is a stark variance from a Criminal proceeding. You see Criminally, its unto the Prosecution to prove their case. However, in many Civil cases, it's up to you to prove to the Judge or Jury that your actions were Justified. It's this shift of Burden, which is why *ZuluShield* is so extraordinarily vital to your Defense. The only way to prove justification for killing another, is to show example after example of why you simply had to do what you did. It's also vitally important to site actual real-world incidents where other reasonably minded people; who were faced with similar circumstances, chose to take a similar course of action in their own defense. Yet in Court you need 'Proof' not examples by mere testimony. What you'll need are actual print-outs or some form of physical, tactile type evidence which you'll present as an example of 'Reasonable Action' and that's exactly what this system provides. With *ZuluShield*, you'll have a plethora of examples and a multitude of avenues of Defense to justify your actions and prove your innocence.

Let's use a Home Invasion Robbery scenario. We'll say the assailant breaks in your residence in the middle of the night and you're startled from your stupor. You fear for the safety of yourself and your family and decide to arm yourself with your handgun. Knowing police are too far away to intercede, you decide to conduct a Safety Clear of your home. During the process of the clear, you confront the assailant who you find standing 15-feet from you in the middle of your living room. Even though you had expected to find him, you were startled by the sight of him. Your heart's pounding and you soon realize this is the real thing. You can't see his hands and can barely make his face due to the darkness. You notice him begin to walk slowly towards you. Knowing that 'Time' itself is NOT on your side, you decide to shoot and in turn kill him.

Most police investigations would find this to be 'Reasonably Justified Force' due to the fact that the assailant broke in at night, when it's likely you'd be home, thereby posing a greater risk to your safety. Police also know just how quickly a simple Cat Burglary can turn violent. Civilly though, the Assailant's family is going to argue up and down that if you would have only turned on a light, told their loved one to leave or just barricaded your family in the back room, while you waited for police, nobody would have needed to be harmed. Basically the Plaintiff throws spaghetti on the wall till one of their arguments sticks. While you typically can't be imprisoned Civilly, you can most certainly lose everything and never be able to regain your status for the remainder of your life. Scenarios like this one are why this happens. Unless of course you prepare ahead of time.

The 'OJ Defense' does NOT work during a Civil trial. In fact, OJ Simpson ended up being found liable for the Wrongful Death of his ex-wife and was hit with a $25-million penalty. Even though he won his Criminal case, it left him completely bankrupt, so the Civil case hit him even harder leaving him completely insolvent and we all know where that lead him.

Your only hope of avoiding a Civil case is to preemptively gather as much data on Self-Defense cases, brainstorm, then document scenario after scenario of how and why the use of Deadly Physical Force is or has already been found to be Reasonable. The goal is to retain this information and counter each individual argument a Plaintiff could make, with a dozen or more reasons why their argument is NOT reasonable and how Courts have already found your actions to be Justified in similar real-world incidents. *ZuluShield* makes this easy and will be an extraordinarily priceless resource and a vital tool which your attorney can use to unequivocally prove your innocence.

Why a preemptive approach is so vital...

Regardless of whether you find yourself in Criminal or Civil Court, your ability to accurately describe exactly why you chose to do what you did is paramount. It's just as vitally important that you eliminate any chance of misunderstanding whatsoever. It's essential that your reasons for said actions are completely understood so as to be found 'Objectively Reasonable' and not simply Subjective by nature. This requires a degree of articulation that most people simply do not have and that can usually only be accomplished through the assistance of an experienced attorney.

Perspectives of Self-Defense are based on conjuncture. Conjuncture is a kaleidoscope of random yet similar assumptions of an outcome that's based on a thought process of past experiences. Perspectives are also composed of an intangible premonition of impending doom due to exposure of the knowledge of similar previous incidents, all woven together to formulate the facts by which you justified such an extreme action. So, your attorney must fully comprehend the gravity and temperature of your past experiences; whether those experiences actually happened to you or in circumstances where you're basing said actions on a someone else's real-life incident. Then they go about measuring the legality of your actions, so as to determine the best ways to formulate the most accurate explanation to the Court. They do so by selecting the 'Exact' vernacular which BEST describes your Defense.

So how do you do this? How does one explain why they did what they did when you don't even know what particular words best define it? You could wait until you've already acted in Self-Defense. You could attempt at that time and while under the most extreme amounts stress, quickly and off-the-cuff, think back to your past experiences and things you've learned. Then verbally describe those concepts to your attorney, while drawing context to the incident in question. This is what most people do but it's far from the most accurate. Sure you may remember particular things of importance, but having the ability to combine it all together so it's presentable and palatable in Court, is an entirely different story all together.

What this system provides is a means of preemptively communicating these facts to your attorney, to afford you the BEST chances of obtaining the most solid legal advice and services, customized to your particular individual needs, without being required to actively think back and remember things from say five, ten or even twenty years in the past. This manual is also specifically designed to give you the most practical means of retaining important data of similar incidents that happened to someone else, which may later actually play an active role in your decision process. *ZuluShield* also provides a similar way of retaining these incidents of Self-Defense, which Courts have previously found to be reasonable. This way you don't have to remember minute facts, times, places or even people involved, all those years later while under enormous stress. All you have to do is flip through your convenient and strategically structured *ZuluShield Archive*.

Let's revisit the Home Invasion Robbery scenario from earlier. Remember the assailant breaks in your residence in the middle of the night and you're startled from your stupor. You decide to grab your firearm and clear your house, when you confront the assailant who's standing in your living room. You're scared and can't see if he's armed or not, decide to shoot and in turn kill him. You determined your course of action for a number of reasons:

1. The person unlawfully entered and is remaining in your home.

2. Its night so you conclude that he must have assumed you'd be home, which means he would have reasonably planned for you being there and although you can't see a weapon, you believe it reasonable under those circumstances that he would have armed himself.

3. You also decided to shoot based on the fact that you know Home Invasion Robberies to be extremely dangerous and unpredictable.

4. You chose NOT to warn or tell the intruder to 'Freeze' because you know from training that 'Action' is always faster than 'Reaction' and you FEARED that by giving the intruder any more time to contemplate an attack, WOULD cost you your life.

5. Now let's say you've come to this conclusion because of a number of incidents in the past which you've seen or read about in the News and one in particular stood out, which you end up specifically siting.

All of this is mixed together and clearly articulates a reasonable basis for your actions and that you reasonably feared that your life and your family's were in grave danger and you were justified in the use of Deadly Physical Force to protect 'Life'. In no time, you're able to give clear articulation supported by tangible facts. Now contrast that with a 'Reactive Defense Strategy' where you're left picking up the pieces while you develop your Defense on-the-fly.

"That's good!" you say, "that's what I want!" Yes, the above mentioned rundown of articulation is wonderful and will undoubtedly keep you out of jail. However, for Court purposes you need much, much more. You need hard facts, something tangible, otherwise its mere conjecture and is far too 'Subjective' by nature. In Court you must present factual detail. The Court needs to know the dates and times of those past incidents you've eluded to as part of your decision process for using force. You must also show why any of that actually relates to the context of your particular Self-Defense claim. Trying to remember all this information and the overwhelming amount of other important facts, all while under the gauntlet of extreme stress, is an uphill battle and the reason why so many people fail so miserably in Court and exactly why they either plead or settle Civilly despite their innocence.

ZuluShield is specifically designed to make your Court proceedings a much easier and more successful experience. With this system you'll not only learn how to effectively articulate example after example, but your attorney will have those examples right there at their fingertips, all strategically organized to give you a bulletproof Legal Defense. Your due diligence today, will pay dividends tomorrow.

Chapter 2

3 Steps to Success

By now, I'm certain you're convinced on the vital importance of developing a Proactive Legal Defense for tomorrow's Deadly Encounter. In this chapter I'm going to show you the 3 steps of success; that if adhered to, will payoff tomorrow. It all comes down to you though, its up to you to take your Legal Defense serious and commit to making it the MOST solid Defense possible.

The number one goal of a Proactive Legal Defense, is finding a way of showing your attorney exactly why you did what you did, back that decision with a myriad of supporting information and facts, as to what lead you to make that decision, and finally for your attorney to fully comprehend what you communicate and find a why of making that palatable in Court. Basically you need to paint a picture that is clearly understood from ANY vantage point.

Think of it like a TV screen. When looking at a clear crisp image on say a 72" flat screen, it's easy to overlook the architecture behind that image. We typically forget that the image is in fact composed of thousands and thousands of individual but individually colored pixels. It's the individuality of their distinct color, how their relationship with one another is organized in concert with those to their left, right, top and bottom and the combined amalgamation of the entire sequence of every pixel, which provides 'One' single particular image, to have 'One' completely common perspective, no matter where you stand in a given room. This is the degree of clarity you MUST speak with.

Effectively articulating your Defense by breaking it down into its individual 'Pixels' then organizing them in a manner which affords EVERYBODY your perspective; at the time of the incident, and for that perspective to be the ONLY image seen no matter who's seeing it at any place in the Court room and for that to be felt and understood in the hearts and minds of the Judge and Jury, is the key to success. The following 3 steps and the chapters that follow, represent the all important pixels you'll need in order to present the most solid Self-Defense case with the highest definition and the greatest degree of clarity.

The Firewall
Attorney Communiqué
What When Mentality

Step 1 (What When Mentality)

The first step in achieving the advantage is to change the way you think. Don't settle for a passive; "If this happens, then I'll do that" type of approach for tomorrow. Instead, develop an adherence to the concept of, 'Not If But When.' Don't merely own a firearm for 'If' something should happen. Rather, actively possess it for WHEN your life WILL be threatened and WHEN you WILL be forced to use it to protect yourself and someone else. It's this mindset that immediately thrusts you into a whole new world of mental preparation. I'm not suggesting you become paranoid of the world around you. However, I am compelling you to prepare for whatever WILL be thrown your way. If you prepare for the worst-case scenario and devise a few 'Reasonably Objective' ways of defeating such an obstacle, then anything less than that should be easily overcome. It's a bit like resistance training. If you train yourself to lift a heavy weight, then pretty soon the lighter ones feel like feathers. The more you lift the fitter you become and the fitter you are, the more capable you are for the challenge.

The 'What When Mentality' translates into: "when I'm confronted by someone while I exit my front door" and "when I'm walking to my car in a dark parking garage and I'm attacked from behind" and "when I'm sitting on my couch and I'm startled by the front door being kicked in" and "when I'm at a stoplight and am confronted by a man with at gun at my driver side window" and "when I'm at the mall with my kids and see a man with a rifle killing people left and right" or "when out at a sports bar enjoying drinks with my friends and a stranger picks a fight with me." These are examples of the depth by which you must take your thought and for each 'When' you need to take the time to formulate at least three different ways of overcoming such an occurrence and finally document this reasoning for each individual set of circumstances.

I'm not by any stretch of the imagination suggesting that any or all of the previous examples are (pull your gun and shoot) scenarios. However, I'm not suggesting they're NOT. What I am saying is committing your mind to 'Forward Thought' affords you the opportunity to think and reason ahead of time. In fact you can take all the time you need today and even ask the advice of your attorney or other experts beforehand, just to make sure you get it right tomorrow. It's this What When Mentality which causes you to take a much more cognitive approach to Firearms Self-Defense. It's the 'When' which forces you to make a decision today because its not a possibility but a 'Probability'. It's a statement, not a question and it's this approach which affords you the MOST well thought, squared-away response possible. It's the 'When' which gives you the best chances of avoiding a legal battle all together because tomorrow you'll be able to employ the MOST reasonable and effective use-of-force possible.

Step 2 (Attorney Communiqué):

Now that you've got your mind thinking right, it's time to take your next proactive step towards securing a solid Defense. The objective of this step is focused on taking the time today to gather vital information; data and facts about your experiences and the experiences of others in the world around you, relating to the topic of Self-Defense, the spread of violent crime and its deadly consequences to victims who don't use Self-Defense, as well as any Court case relating to the topics of Self-Defense. What you'll do here is take the 'What When Mentality' and use real-world, factually tangible events and marry those to the development of the habitual practice of documenting these facts for your future Legal Defense. Think of this step as a continual seek and destroy mission. The purpose is to provide your attorney with as much tangibility as entirely possible. Your goal is to select incidents, data and information you believe may be of importance to your future Defense. You do this today, so your attorney will not only be able to give you the BEST legal advice tomorrow but also have the capability of customizing a bulletproof Legal Defense should you require it.

The idea here is a concept you've probably never heard before, but it's a strategy that will prove to provide you with the most probable chance of avoiding Court altogether. You'll be composing what I term as an 'Attorney Communiqué.' It's important that you fully grasp the gravity of such a concept, for it represents the philosophical foundation of *ZuluShield*. It's also the most ingenious method of preemptively protecting vital information from the discovery process, to assure it's kept private and completely confidential between you and your attorney. This is huge! Trust me your attorney will thank you later.

Basically, you're going to compose a pre-structured, strategically designed system of correspondence between you and your attorney. This correspondence will remain private and confidential so it can be used, by your attorney to give you the most appropriate legal service required, should you actually be forced to act in Self-Defense. I can't stress enough just how critical it is for you to understand the strategic importance of this concept. Don't worry, while this may sound complicated, the process is actually straight forward and easily accomplished. I've taken the hassle and guesswork out of it. For the most part you simply fill in the blanks and follow a few basic instructions. The hard parts already done for you, once you get used to the process, it'll be as easy as tying your shoes.

After putting your 'What When' thinking-cap on, you soon realize the likelihood that you <u>WILL</u> one day be confronted by a person who <u>WILL</u> pose a Deadly Threat to you or someone else. This unfortunate circumstance <u>WILL</u> force you to make a decision on how you <u>WILL</u> defend yourself and or a third-party. <u>WILL</u> either make your defense with your hands or you <u>WILL</u> be forced to use a weapon. It's only logical from here to conclude that this circumstance <u>WILL</u> place you in a very precarious position and <u>WILL</u> expose you to Criminal and or Civil liability. Hence you require 'Legal Advice' on exactly how to deal with this exposure and you have a few very important questions to ask your attorney relating to the legality of your actions.

If you've noticed, I'm overemphasizing a few vitally important words. It's essential that you catch on to the fact that you've already determined what WILL happen. It's not 'If' but WHEN and you've decided to initiate a system of communicating your questions and perspectives to your attorney. The objective is not only to arrive at the BEST solution, but to find solutions with a solid legal backing.

As far as the law and determining foreseeable liability, there's no greater resource than that of a competent attorney. Due to the complexity of both Criminal and Civil Law, it is commonly accepted and assumed that a person seek-out the legal advice of a certified attorney prior to any legal proceeding. In fact, the expectation of legal counsel goes so far back in time that it is infused in the very DNA of centuries old 'Common Law.'

Because the 'Attorney Client Relationship' has been recognized for centuries, there are particular protections, which are of great interest to you should you find yourself in the crosshairs of a Self-Defense legal battle. There is one though, which far precedes all the rest and that is the 'Attorney Client Privilege.' While this privilege is not necessarily cut and dry and there are some variances from Federal to State and from State to State Courts, there is a manner in which you can take advantage of this privilege in a way that most people have never thought of. It's this technique which will prove to be so pivotal to your Defense; even years from now, when you face your very own Self-Defense legal battle.

Now it's important to understand that this technique is a 'Privilege' not a 'Right.' The last thing you want is to have the information contained in this system, seized as a result of a Search Warrant during a Criminal Investigation. The information you retain in this Communiqué is essential in determining the most accurate legal advice. So maintaining its confidentiality is paramount. There is no independent Constitutional Amendment affirming the Attorney Client Privilege. It is NOT inalienable. However, as mentioned above, it is an integral ingredient of Common Law and has been since the start. So it's as close to any guarantee as you're going to get.

The foundational understanding is that by providing a person a particular sense of privacy and security between them and their attorneys, it automatically facilitates a standard of 'Honesty' and encourages a person to be forthcoming during their interactions with the Court. Honesty is the most elemental and essentially indispensable ingredient of our Justice System. It's impossible for any Court to truly determine what's 'Right' without consistent honesty and transparency on the parts of both the Prosecution and the Defense. And so, to cultivate trustworthiness, Courts have a history of keeping conversations between an attorney and their client, completely private, confidential and undiscoverable. This means no matter how badly the Prosecutor wants to know exactly what you've told your attorney; in hopes they may uncover a confession on your part, Courts have the historical Past-Practice of denying such attempts and instead place the burden on the Prosecutor to prove guilt based on evidence and the elements of a crime.

Every Court from Federal on down to local, recognizes, understands and fully supports the benefit of sustaining this privilege. There are also Federal and

State Laws, like the 'Attorney Client Privilege Protection Act' giving definition to this concept while also providing a fare bit of guaranteed protection. Our nation's highest Court has also made a handful of decisions over the years concerning this privilege and offer even more guidance and clarity. There is however a fare amount of misunderstanding on this topic. Despite what you may have been told, not all conversations with your attorney are protected. So it is critical that you pay special attention to the details and know what is protected and how you can assure the information you retain in this system remains confidential.

As mentioned previously, the last thing you want is for this communication to be seized by law enforcement during a Search Warrant. This would occur as a result of a fact-finding-mission on the part of authorities. Remember, they're investigating a very serious crime which could rise to homicide. In some circumstances they may desire to search your residence in hopes that they uncover possible motives and or evidence that may otherwise be concealed. They will also attempt to determine who you are, what books you read, what websites you frequent and other probes to better understand what your political views may be, if you have an axe to grind or if you have connections to criminal entities. All of this information is extremely important later in Court, should they determine a crime has been committed. Should that be the case, it's vital that the data contained in this communication is not lost or locked away in a police evidence locker. The intent of this communication is for legal advice between you and your attorney and will contain a treasure-trove of very important pieces of information your attorney will need in order to give you the BEST advice. So assuring that it's protected and readily available to you following your use of Self-Defense, is paramount.

In order for communication to be considered 'Protected' there are a few elements it must have and they must share each of the following four elements:

1. Be initiated by the client to a certified attorney who holds a recognized license to practice Law by The Bar.

2. Be for purposes of receiving some type of legal advice and or other legal services.

3. Be completely private and confidential by nature.

4. Come after the retention of an attorney has been made for this protection to take effect.

Let's explore these elements. On Page (1) of this manual, you will find a legal notice. The reason for this notice is to notify law enforcement and anybody else, exactly what your intent is pertaining to the contents of this manual and its associated components. The fact that it is found on the very first page makes for an extremely strong argument as to what this manual actually represents. The notice plainly outlines the intent of this manual and speaks to each of the four required elements, which in turn communicates that you intend for this manual and its associated components to remain 'Protected Communication.' As you will see, the notice makes it very clear that this is not merely a book with notes but it embodies an actual form and method of communication between yourself and your attorney. It's extremely important that you actually read, print and sign your name and adhere to the guidelines of this notice. Remember, if you make reference to this manual in the future, it is *"a private and confidential communication between you and your attorney"* and must NEVER be shared with ANYONE other than your attorney under ANY circumstances.

The first element is pretty straight forward. You must prove 'You' initiated this communication. That's pretty easily argued by the explanation of the notice, your printed name and your signature as such.

The second element is also easily proved by the notice itself because it clearly states the intent of everything that follows, which is intended to be used for purposes of obtaining "Legal Advice" and or "Legal Services" from your attorney.

The third element is also affirmed by the notice. I call this 'Pleading the 4th.' The Fourth Amendment to the United States Constitution pertains to the topic of 'Governmental Search and Seizure.' The notice basically acts as a buffer between you and the Government for everything that follows to include your notes, means by which you archive your data and anything associated with this communication from here on. Even during Civil trials, should the Court; 'Government', order this information to be 'Discoverable', a clear argument can be made by your attorney that such an order by 'Government' would be a clear violation of the Fourth Amendment of the United States Constitution.

However, it's vital you understand that in order to maintain its confidentiality, you must NEVER share or discuss the details of this communication with ANYONE other than your attorney. This even includes friends and family.

The last element is very important, in order for the protection to be put in play; you must 'First' retain an attorney. Step Three will explain just how easy and inexpensive it is to accomplish.

If done correctly, any communication from here, between you and your attorney; which can be tied to this 'Attorney Communiqué, is and will remain protected and undiscoverable. Chapter (4) will give you an in-depth rundown on just how easy and straightforward the *ZuluShield* process is and how easily it can be accomplished and just how simple it is for your attorney to utilize.

Step 3 (The Firewall):

Before I continue, it's vitally important that you <u>DO NOT</u> ignore or skip this most crucial step. In order to take FULL advantage of the protections already available to you; which can save your bacon tomorrow, you <u>NEED</u> to take heed to what follows.

I know what you're thinking, attorney retainers are expensive and you don't have the time. In most cases you'd be right however, NOT in this case and you NEED to take the time in this case. The intent of this step is not that you rush off and throw down thousands of dollars on some random attorney. Quite the contrary actually. The goal is to be 'Selective'. To locate an attorney in your immediate area who's been successful with Self-Defense claims. Then, meet with that attorney, present the *ZuluShield* concept inform them that the services you require will be for future Legal Defense, should you be forced to act in Self-Defense. Next, you work with them to structure an inexpensive customized open-ended retainer

In this day and age, insurance companies will sell insurance for just about anything. Heck you can't even check-out of the big-box electronic stores anymore without them attempting to push some sort of three-year protection plan on you. Think of the Attorney Retainer as a type of Self-Defense Insurance. If you knew with any certainty today, that you'll be involved in a serious car crash tomorrow, you'd be rushing off right now to get the very BEST car and disability insurance you could possibly find?

The concept is that you've retained your attorney for tomorrow's legal battle and that you have initiated an 'Attorney Communiqué' by which you will express your perspectives, give information, show real-life examples, give facts and in turn use this data as a means of 'Telling Your Story' for exactly 'Why' you chose to defend yourself or someone else. For the most part your attorney's actual involvement prior to a Self-Defense incident will be limited. However, it's important that you understand that along the way, you may come across legal questions as you play the 'What When Game'. When you arrive at those legal questions, it is highly suggested that you pick your attorney's brain to arrive at an answer that's consistent with the laws you'll eventually be judged by. Now if you're like anyone, the last thing you want to do is spend money asking questions. However, attorneys are experts in Law, its vital that should you have legitimate legal questions along the way, that you invest in finding answers today, that can actually assist in your Defense tomorrow.

Why does it benefit an attorney to agree to an indefinite or customized retainer? The same reason Insurances companies sell insurance. From the perspective of the attorney, it's highly unlikely they'll ever have to actually assist you with in-depth legal services. Equally appealing, should you ever actually require their service, the types of service you'll need, will most certainly cost a pretty penny. Meaning, when their services are required, they will most definitely make a substantial amount of money providing those services. So to the attorney it's easy money and a possible jackpot. It's in their best interests to take your money, its really that simple.

However, like mentioned previously, it's not just any attorney that's suited for the task ahead. To benefit fully from the potency of this manual, you should take the time to research a few successful Defense Attorneys in your area and select one who's done well with Self-Defense claims. Again, I'm not suggesting you fork-out thousands of dollars. In fact, when presented with the *ZuluShield* concept, many Defense Attorneys can structure a customized open-ended retainer for a few hundred dollars. Think about it, you've undoubtedly spent more investing in your firearm and equipment. Doesn't it make since to back that up should you actually have to use your firearm in the real-world?

When you finally select your attorney, they will likely request a consultation meting. In that meeting they'll hear what kinds of services you're requesting and work with you to develop a retainer which works for you. During this consultation its important that you communicate the following:

1. Explain to them that you have initiated a Proactive Legal Defense should you be forced to defend your life or someone else's.

2. Show them the *ZuluShield* concept and encourage them to contact me should they have particular questions about the system.

3. That you'll be utilizing the *ZuluShield* system as an Attorney Communiqué and intend it to be used as a means of telling your story to them and that you fully intend this Communiqué remain fully confidential.

4. Next, inform them that you wish to retain them for legal advice and services pertaining to said 'Future' Legal Defense should you be forced to defend your life or someone else's.

5. That you require an indefinite open-ended retainer for the possibility of this occurrence.

6. That you would also wish to be afforded the ability to periodically ask questions or pick their brains along the way should you require clarity on a particular legal question pertaining to your Proactive Legal Defense and would like a payment schedule to be structured for these periodic exchanges.

7. Inform them that you fully intend to call on them should you actually be required to defend your life or someone else's.

Failing to properly follow this most vital step, could in fact compromise the integrity of your Legal Defense all together. The essence of this manual is that it remains legally recognized and Protected Communiqué between you and your attorney and that it remains completely confidential and private all the way through future legal proceedings.

By failing to following this step, two extremely devastating outcomes are possible:

1. All of your data and in turn your Legal Defense, could end up being locked away in a police evidence locker following a search warrant.

2. If this were to occur, it's conceivable that this data could be used by the Prosecution to develop solid 'Counters' to each and every piece of evidence you use to support your innocence.

However, following this step affords the following:

1. Nearly insurmountable protection under Attorney Client Privilege to assure that your Proactive Legal Defense remains confidential.

2. An immediate point-of-contact of extremely important expert legal questions, pertaining to Self-Defense.

3. A competent attorney already on stand-by should you be forced to defend yourself or someone else.

4. An attorney who's already familiar with you and your Defense strategy and who knows exactly where to start from when they receive the call.

Remember, the crux of this system is to provide its user with a straightforward method of initiating a Proactive Legal Defense and that this Defense be the best, most bulletproof Defense possible today. So you're not scattering to formulate a last-minute Defense tomorrow. *ZuluShield* is specifically designed to offer a density of tangible evidentiary substance, which will give your attorney plenty of ways to present your case. However, to take full advantage of this system, you must take the time now and invest in the protection a simple attorney retainer affords you. Having an attorney on stand-by may just make all the difference in the world.

Chapter 3

Force Science

Solid combatives training is a key element in any effective Self-Defense Response. To survive the battle, you MUST gain effective proficiency in the 'Kinesis' of the 'Fight'. To when the Legal War that follows, which is what *ZuluShield* is designed to afford, can only be accomplished if your fight was carried-out 'Reasonably' and within the confines of the Law.

Too often armed-citizens take a cavalier approach to the likelihood of using their firearms in Self-Defense. They do so without properly thinking 'Through' the process of Self-Defense. What happens is they quite often set themselves up for failure and in many cases an overreaction.

The intent of this chapter is to communicate just how crucial it is that you become well versed with the Science behind conflict, so you can both develop practical and reliable Combative Responses, but also so you become fully aware of the 'Parameters' or Laws of Combat, which are as real as the Laws of Physics.

While it's vitally important that you marry the concepts of what's called 'Force Science' to your combatives training, its also important to know how the Laws of Combat can be used to protect you in Court. Most people are completely ignorant about conflict and have completely unrealistic understandings of this most chaotic happening, as well as completely unreasonable expectations as to how a given person should react and perform while in the heat of Combat itself.

Its this ignorance of 'Fact' which spells disaster for many Self-Defense claims. The reason is that most people; to include the Judge and Jury, have no concept whatsoever about the relationship between Action vs. Reaction and Combat Gravity and just how much they impact one's decision making process while under attack. For instance, the average person would expect you to give a person armed with a knife, a bit longer before you end up shooting them. In both cases, the average person would even expect you to 'Wait' until your attacker actually overtly threatens the use of their weapon before you shoot. A simple lesson in Action vs. Reaction will put that senseless expectation to rest. Combine this with an in depth look at the unique Stress Dump people experience during times of attack, will make it very clear that 'Time' is a commodity you simply CAN'T sacrifice

Similarly, the vast majority of people haven't the foggiest idea as to just how overwhelming an actual fight for your life is. There are so many factors which play into your particular Self-Defense Response, which will completely go overlooked unless you educate not just the Judge and or Jury but your attorney as well, about why the Laws of Combat MUST be considered when determining if your actions were justified.

A perfect example of this is the 'Overkill' concept and shooting someone in their back. I bring this up again because it happens so often. Let's go back to that Home Invasion scenario form Chapter (1). Now let's say you confront your attacker who is completely unarmed. While pointing your firearm at him, you order him to drop to the ground, show you his hands and wait until police arrive. However, this bad guy's not having it. Instead, he charges you, knowing you're not going to shoot an unarmed man. The result is a fight for your life and you struggle to maintain control of your firearm. At some point you realize you're losing the battle and have no other option but to shoot the unarmed attacker off of you. The fight is so real by now that you can literally taste your impending death. You make the decision to shoot, and the world around you goes foggy. As you come to your senses you realize that you're still alive and you have shot and killed your unarmed attacker, who's laying in a pool of blood on your living room floor.

During the Forensics Investigation, police determine you shot your unarmed attacker (6) times. To your shock, they determined that only (2) of those gunshot wounds were to the unarmed attacker's front and that the remaining (4) wounds were to his side and back. On top of this, they determine the cause of death was a gunshot wound which entered his back and exploded his heart. So basically he died because you shot him in his back.

Because the circumstances are so foggy, you are unable to effectively articulate just how dynamic the fight for your life actually was. For whatever reason, you were unable to find the right words to explain to police that when you decided to shoot, the attacker was on top of you attempting to gain control of the firearm and that when you shot, you were also on the ground, on your back and in the process of scooting him off and away form you. What you didn't know was at the same moment, your unarmed attack was making for a hasty retreat and had already begun the process of turning and running away from you. The result of his decision to retreat at the exact moment that you had made your decision to shoot, meant that the majority of your rounds hit him while he was on the run. Thereby making it scientifically impossible to 'Stop' shooting.

To an investigator and most people, seeing the gunshot wounds could easily be misunderstood as an indication that you unlawfully shot a fleeing unarmed Cat Burglar in his back. It goes without saying, just how complicated a case like this could be and just how vulnerable you would be to actually being convicted of Manslaughter or even Murder.

What if I told you 'Force Science' could put this whole case to rest? That's the intent of this chapter, to give you the knowledge today to develop both a Combatives Response to a Deadly Threat and a better balanced Proactive Legal Defense for said response, which is backed by the Science which determines ALL when it comes to a fight for your life.

So what is it anyway...

Force Science is the study of the most extreme forms of physical conflict between humans known as 'Deadly Force Encounters'. Force Science dissects the dynamics associated with Combat to identify and measure physiological and psychological effects, which may be common from one person to another.

Force Science is a frailly new discipline, which began in the early 1970s. The intent was twofold:

1. The Special Operations Community wanted to find ways to increase a warfighters' overall potency on the battlefield and identify ways to pass this on to the regular army.

2. Top military brass were concerned with the overwhelming number of service members returning from Vietnam, who suffered from extreme psychological disorders. The extremely high numbers of Psych Casualties were most alarming and far greater than any previous conflict. They wanted to figure out what if anything had changed; in terms of Combat, and exactly how Combat; itself, effected the average warfighter.

The long and short is that scientists found exactly what they were searching for, but they also uncovered a treasure trove of information that's completely changed how we approach Combat today. However, it took some time for scientist, psychologist and doctors to catch up to a whole new way of thinking.

Twenty years later; in the 1990s, two main groups took this research to a whole new level and made it the science we know today. KILLOLOGY RESEARCH GROUP and the FORCE SCIENCE INSTITUTE ® are two completely independent and unbiased-based groups comprised of scientists, doctors, psychologist and tactical experts, who focus on the physiological and psychological effects of Deadly Force Encounters. Man has been in Combat since Cane and Able, yet astonishingly, the 'Science' behind Combat has been pretty much hit and miss, (pun intended) until the advent of the above mentioned groups.

They were the first to connect the dots and fill in the gaps from the more archaic research of the 1970s. They were able to identify patterns and extrapolate probable outcomes to give us a much better understand of exactly what to expect when we're faced with a Deadly Threat. What their research has found tells us that we've been doing it wrong all along. Sadly, we've been training to LOSE not to win.

Combat Gravity...

If there is one thing the study of Force Science has revealed, it would be that there exists a myriad of unavoidable and common effects, which everybody experiences. Combat itself has a very distinct impact on how a person will actually physically respond while threatened. This impact is vastly different than how a person acts under ANY other circumstances, other than during the most extreme life or death situations. The sum of these effects represent what I call the 'Laws of Combat'. These laws can be likened to Sir Isaac Newton's 'Laws of Physics'. The mere existence of Combat, has a measurable and defined affect on man. Regardless of race, nationality, gender or physical composition, there are a handful of common effects of Combat, which cannot be averted.

Think of it in terms of 'Gravity'. Everybody knows the affect of gravity when it relates to our ability to maneuver here on Earth. It's what keeps our feet to the ground, our constant. In the same way, Combat has its own gravitational force. There are physiological and psychological realties that affect every man, woman or child who experiences Combat.

The reality is that we all experience extremely similar effects during a struggle for our existence. While each individual effect is not guaranteed, every human being engaged in Combat, will experience the majority of them to one extreme or another. While these effects are completely unavoidable, their influence can be dramatically reduced to a much more manageable degree. Science has shown that we can pre-condition our minds and in turn our bodies; beforehand, to experience 'Combat Gravity' with less overall affect on our ability to navigate its waters.

An analogy of this concept can be derived from the conditioning an Astronaut undergoes prior to their travel into outer space. Over a life of experiencing the effects of Gravity here on Earth, their bodies have developed their own harmonic balance. If abruptly thrust into space and placed on the Moon, a person would experience great discomfort and fear without proper preparation, since they would end up bouncing from one side to the other. To this day Astronauts practice simulated Low Gravity Training, so they're adequately prepared for the effects of said Gravity on the Moon or Space in general. Something as simple as drinking water in Space, can be a very daunting task and extremely difficult to complete while in Space. Yet on Earth this most basic function, which most of us master by the age of (4), is taken for granted here on Earth. Similar basic physical functions associated with using a firearm while under attack, are just as much an out-of-this-world experience as drinking water from a cup, in an almost zero gravity environment like that of the International Space Station.

Just as the Moon is a world away from our experiences here on Earth, Combat is as distant our everyday lives as Mars or better yet Pluto. In the same way, Force Science has shown that anyone can prep for tomorrow's battle and develop natural responses to afford them the most positive outcome.

An example on how poor training can completely sabotage one's ability to win during the 'Act' of Combat, can be found in something as simple as how they stand during training. Stance is one of the most overlooked aspects of firearms training, yet it provides the entire base for your Physical Response. For the most part people initially acquire a stance that looks tactical cool like the 'Isosceles Stance'. But soon and usually within a few short minutes, their stance becomes more of a flat-footed, weight on heals Weaver Stance. What happens is they lose focus of the 'Crouch' and forward lean required for an effective Isosceles Stance and quickly get tired due to muscle fatigue. What results is the entirety of the rest of their training is performed from a completely different base, which completely effects overall accuracy. The laziness and poor habitual manner of their stance in training, is then encoded in their brain as Muscle Memory through the procedural aspects of their training.

Interestingly, Force Science research clearly shows that EVERYONE who actually perceives an immediately attacking lethal threat, will instinctively assume a squatted crouch, identical to that of the Modified Isosceles shooting stance. No matter how well you've training and no matter how elite your profession may be, this is latterly an innate physical reaction that CAN'T be overridden. A great example of this can be seen in the video footage of then President Reagan's attempted assassination on March 30th 1981. During this real-world deadly attack EVERY single individual is seen assuming an 'Oh Shi Crouch' directly proceeding John Hinckley Junior's initial shots.

What's even more interesting is that each and every person immediately present did the same exact thing regardless of their previous training or their current physical responsibility. From reporter, to staff, to regular police officers to the elite team of Reagan's Secret Service Detail, each and every person crouched and maintained that crouch throughout their following Physical Response. Remember, members of a Secret Serve Presidential Security Detail, undergo a degree of unheard of pre-training and continued training that could easily be likened to the practice of a Religion. Even with all their training, each Secret Service member crouched in the same fashion and even paused for about the same amount of time, prior to putting into motion their Defensive Response.

The reality is that during attack you WILL assume a 'Modified Isosceles Stance' throughout the incident regardless of your previous training. If Force Science has proven that this is as much of a reality as Gravity is to the Law of Physics, then why do so many people waste so much time shooting from a Weaver or any other type of shooting stance? Your shooting stance is your 'Base' it determines and galvanizes the overall integrity of all other aspects of fighting which shooting is but 'One' portion. Maintaining proper stance through the entirety of your training will assure that all the other physical movements you hone during that training evolution, are not wasted and are built on a sure foundation that's consistent with the Laws of Combat and don't attempt to defy the Laws of Physics. Understanding something so simple yet so vitally important as 'Stance' during training, highlights just why an adequate grasp of the topic of Force Science is so essential if you want to 'Win' tomorrow's battle. Winning is first accomplished through the 'pre'-study of conflict.

The mind, a terrible thing to waste...

Our brains define us and set us apart from all other living beings. The totality, function and overall capabilities they offer are inconceivable. Neuroscientists are still uncovering the secrets and wonder behind how our brains develop and function. Our brains are truly our greatest asset. Yet, in times of great crisis they can often become our greatest obstacle.

Force Science researchers have consistently shown that our ability to manage 'Combat Stress' is directly derived from how our minds process the concepts of this stress beforehand. It's all about pre-conditioning. In fact, our success is completely dependent upon our mind's ability to formulate an instantaneous response absent cognitive thought. Just as our brain's continually cause our lungs to expand and contract without thought, so too must we have a pre-wired solution for tomorrow's battle. This starts by understanding the processes of our physiology and psychology and how they're affected during

Combat. Similar to how an Olympic Athlete utilizes Hyperbaric Chamber Training to pre-condition their lungs for the extreme stressors of such a high level of competition, so too must you pre-condition the physiology and psychology of your mind for Combat.

Fight, Flight or Freeze...

Over the course of our lives, our brains have subconsciously developed one of three instantaneous responses to an immediate and Deadly Threat. We will either 'Fight' our Threat with all our might, 'Flee' from it as fast as humanly possible or we will completely shut down and 'Freeze' like a deer caught in the headlights. This is also known as 'Combat Paralysis', which can last anywhere from seconds or minutes and can easily lead to a medical state of shock.

Our brains are designed to develop and operate on two parallel planes. During times of grave danger and when faced with a threat to our very existence, our brains revert back to the most primitive forms of function.

1. The first and most common plane, I like to call the 'Intelligent Brain'. It's where we live 99.99% of our lives. It's the cognitive and intellectually creative form of us. This operation is achieved through the cooperative interaction of our Prefrontal Cortex with both our brain's right and left hemispheres.

   - To better understand this, our Intelligent Brain is like our desktop computer. It's comprised of all that makes our computer different than the next. It is made up of its operating system and background functions, the main hard-drive, auxiliary drives and the multitude of custom software suites.

2. The second is much more primitive than the Intelligent Brain. I call this the 'Caveman Brain' or the Amygdala. It's mainly comprised of all our basic body functions; the innate processes our brain makes on its own, which maintain all 11 basic body function systems, like those of our nervous and circulatory systems. It also consists of an extremely small sampling of our Intelligent Brain's ability to problem solve.

   - To better understand this, our Caveman Brain is like our desktop computer's master default, the archaic DOS or C Prompt. No Windows OS, no software, just code.

   - Many so called Tactical Experts have training methods which fall apart during real-life Combat because they designed their methods on an Intellectual footing requiring the use of one's 'Intelligent' cognitive brain function. However, during the polar shift of Combat; where our brains revert back to Caveman function, all those 'Intellectual' possesses go out the window. In Combat you're left with basic computer code, while all those fancy dancy high-tech tactical sexy software applications end up crashing. What you should be doing is learning to be a Combat Computer IT Analyst because that's exactly what you'll need when someone tries to kill you tomorrow and you're faced with the complexities of the unavoidable Combat Computer Code Crash.

Due to genetics and early childhood influences, our Caveman Brains accumulate a mixture of automated responses which are immediately fired when faced with grave danger. This is that small sampling of intellectual problem solving discussed above. When faced with a problem our Caveman Brain throws an extremely primitive solution at it. It really is basic Addition & Subtraction though; it's nowhere near the level of Trigonometry or even Basic Algebra. These automated, pre-programmed, responses are completely innate and instinctive. They're an instantaneous function requiring almost zero cognitive processing whatsoever.

Similar to our body's homeostasis; how it regulates and maintains the perfect PH balance, our brains develop their own form of psychoneuro-homeostasis. Over a lifelong of external influences and experiences, our brains establish a physiological and physiological balance. When balanced, this state of being enables our Intelligent Brains to function with ease in relation to the world around us. However, when faced with impending death, this balance is violently thrown upside-down. At that moment our Caveman Brain floods our systems with a cocktail of the most potent hormones and chemicals. The effects of this mind altering chemical cocktail greatly affects our body's response to the perceived Threat and ultimately determines our overall ability to respond to the Threat(s) or whether we Fight, Flee or end-up Freeze.

Top Secret...

When faced with a Deadly Threat to our very existence, our brains feverishly search for a folder titled 'Top Secret'. This folder holds the solution to our immediate problem. The trouble arises when our brains experiences the polar shift; mentioned previously, as it goes from using the Intelligent Brain to our primitive Caveman Brain. It's at that moment when our secretary; our brain's Amygdala, grabs the first folder she can get her hands on and throws it at the problem. The probability that she will retrieve the particular individual folder, which contains your specifically tailored solution for that particular problem, is completely dependent upon how you've already organized, correlated and filed that folder beforehand. When it comes to the use of a weapon in response to an attacking threat; how you respond, is completely depended upon the degree and quality of Procedural Memory Encoding you've performed beforehand.

Our brains are like huge storage vaults capable of storing a life's long accumulation of information and experiences. For the most part we organize these banks of information in similar fashion to that of a filing system. For Combat experts, this system is as sophisticated as the vault like industrial catalogs like those you'd find at a courthouse or museum.

Most people however, file their information in a much less technical manner. This would more closely resemble an everyday two drawer filing cabinet. Over time our brains develop habits of storage, utilizing different kinds of coding and correlating. Some folders are red while others are blue. Some folders go to the top drawer while others live in the bottom. Some are situated to the left while others are stored to the right. In an everyday world; while experience everyday experiences with low stress, your Intelligent Brain can typically locate nearly any folder by memory of where it was last stored. This is due to the process of Cognitive Thought, which is the brain's overall cooperative effort of all its parts.

Ninety-nine point nine-nine percent of Westerners live their lives in an ultra state of peace. In fact, most Westerners will go a lifetime without being physically confronted let alone have someone actually try and kill them. It's important to understand this because just as our Intelligent Brain develops habits of process, our Caveman Brain does as well. The brain is a muscle and like any muscle, if it's not used, it becomes weak. The down side to our peace filled lives is that our Caveman Brain hardly if ever gets its workout in. So when death comes knocking, our Amygdala is left with the daunting task of finding that 'One' perfect solution for an out-of-this-world problem, amongst the clutter of all the other files, piled up around her. This is where the right kind of training makes all the difference and is precisely why the 'Right' kind of training is so essential.

Our Intelligent Brain utilizes the vastness of the Prefrontal Cortex; which is about the size of your fist, to calculate its solutions for the world around it. In contrast, our Caveman Brain uses an area the size of a pea, the Amygdala. That tiny, barely legible portion of the otherwise vastness of the rest of our brain, that's what our Caveman Brain uses to formulate its response to a Deadly Encounter. That tiny, insignificant dot is the most significantly momentous apparatuses in your entire body. This is what WILL determine how you respond to Deadly Threats. Placing the 'Right' information in an appropriately marked folder during training and storing it in the proper spot, that's what will make all the difference tomorrow. It's this tiny portion of our brain; the Amygdala, that has become the focal point of Force Science. It's this extremely miniscule region of the human brain which gets all the attention. Your ability to overcome tomorrow's Deadly Threat is dependent upon how well you understand this process and how well you 'Condition' and encode a pre-programmed response. Proper conditioning is only achieved through proper training. However, it's not just about 'Training' but the 'Right' kind of training makes this possible.

Most of us place the cart before the horse. We spend a small fortune on that perfect gun, which by all means is guaranteed to stop any bad guy dead in his tracks, right? Wrong! From time to time we set out on a pilgrimage to Tactical Mecca, where we hewn and ready our hands for battle by plinking at cardboard silhouettes or even glass bottles. We then return home and go about our lives as normal. Rarely do we ever actually take the time to stop and 'Think Through' the physiology and psychology of conflict. Neurologists go to school first. Ninety-five percent of their time is spent in books and lecture halls before they ever touch a human brain, let alone begin to cut into one. The kinesis of battle is useless if your brain hasn't been conditioned in the process of selecting the appropriate Tactical Response under the extreme stresses of Combat.

Taking the time to study Force Science and memorizing the scientific Laws of Combat will pay dividends tomorrow. Learning first what your body WILL do, will save you from spending tons of wasted time at the firearms range, inadvertently conditioning and encoding the 'Wrong' tactics for the wrong response.

Warning Apocalyptic Tsunami Ahead!!!

What's all the hype about? What's the big deal? You're ready you say? Oh yes, because you have a 1911 .45 ACP by your side at all times. You're ready for anything....

The truth? Physical confrontations with firearms is the most fluidly dynamic environment you will ever know. The overwhelming and unavoidable tidal wave of physiological and psychological effects, rates up there with an Apocalyptic Tsunami. Armed confrontations aren't action movies or video games and they're no 3 Gun match. There are no do-overs and EVERY error is immediately accompanied by a devastatingly lethal consequence.

Most armed citizens foolishly assume they're defensive firearms abilities are suffice. Many think that because they grew-up around firearms, carry one everywhere they go or because they're an expert 3 Gun competitor; they actually believe whole heartedly, they're ready for Combat. The problem lays in their ignorance of 'Fact' and of the unavoidable troubles which lurk ahead. They simply have no clue of the deluge that will wash over them like the worst kind of tidal wave imaginable. They aren't prepared for, or even aware of, the concept of 'Combat Gravity' nor are have the conditioned themselves to react appropriately in spite of the apocalyptic effects of Combat Stress.

For instance:

Action vs. Reaction:

1. The average untrained attacker can achieve a (90%) hit ratio on their prey, while the average untrained defender can only achieve upwards of around a (17-20%) hit ratio in response?

2. Statistics show that 90% of real-world shootings involve multiple rounds being fired and the average untrained person can shoot (4) rounds per-second. That's right, I said an "Untrained" person can shoot (4) rounds per-second.

3. Action is <u>ALWAYS</u> faster than reaction, it's a scientific fact. It takes the average human (0.30) seconds to simply react to a change in their environment. That's merely identifying the existence of 'Change', NOT reacting to said change. Now begins the daunting task of 'Reaction'. Given the overwhelming Stress Cocktail associated with any deadly attack, it takes a minimum of (0.53) more seconds to overcome and process the initial shock & awe of that attack. Then after all that; at (0.83) seconds, you can actually begin to implement some type of a physical response. Meaning, its not until (0.83) seconds into the fight that your brain tells your hand to move towards your holster.

4. Now consider the totality of the relationship between Action vs. Reaction, physics and your ability to survive the attack. The problem presented is a bad guy who's threatened or is actually using a gun against you. You're already drastically behind the Eight Ball. To survive you must identify the Threat, formulate a response, and then implement said response. As mentioned previously you're likely to sustain between (6.52 – 10.88) hits before you send your first round. If you don't believe this statistic, YouTube the 1981 President Reagan Assassination Attempt. You'll see that John Hinckley Jr. was able to get (6) rounds off, before some of the Worlds most highly trained and capable individuals were able to finally subdue him.

5. This real-world Deadly Encounter is a perfect example because it gives you a snapshot of the cross-section of tactically minded persons present, from the horribly inept reporters and advisors and press sectaries to the elite of the elite

Secret Service Presidential Detail members. It took each of these people so much time to respond that John Hinckley Jr. was able to shoot (6) times in (1.7) seconds, standing (10) feet away from President Reagan. His first shot was a headshot of all things. Four of his (6) shots hit multiple people including Reagan all before he could be subdued. It's only certain Reagan would have been hit more would he not have had an entourage of people immediately present to protect his life. You can rest assure, you WON'T have a Secret Service Detail protecting you when you're attacked.

6. Remerging that bullets don't discriminate between right or wrong, friend or foe, victim or criminal, the reality is that molten hot, razor-sharp, metal objects will likely tare through your body at nearly 1,200 fps. This will cause profuse bleeding and immediately begin the ultimate shutdown of the majority of your overall bodily functions. It's only after this, that science shows that you're humanly capable to draw your weapon and begin the uphill battle of defending your life. Does that concern you? Does it make your stomach turn? It most certainly should. This is why the 'Right' kind of training makes all the difference beforehand.

Close Quarters Battles (C.Q.B.) / Proximity to Threat:

1. Distance equals time. The shorter the distance the less time one has to perceive an attack, react and then overcome the perceived deadly attack.

2. Distance also affects accuracy. Since you're reacting to attack, proximity is NOT your friend. The closer your Threat is, the less accurate he needs to be to achieve lethal hits. If your Threat is completely inept at 25 yards and couldn't even place one round on paper, at two or three feet, it's entirely possible that he'll score a possible and each of his rounds will rip through you before you even react.

3. At close proximity a number of other factors are immediately present. For instance, you can touch, feel, smell and even taste your Threat. The aroma of his body odor, the clamminess of his skin, the perplexing and paralyzing gaze of his lifeless thousand-yard stare. An up close and personal struggle for life with another human being is simply unmatched. It's daunting, spooky and emotionally unsettling even for the most experienced among us.

The Stress Cocktail:

1. **Fear (The Human Phobia of Death)**: The greatest most unavoidable innate reaction to a Deadly Threat is our natural fear of death. While some can learn to dilute and decrease the affect of this reaction, most people will be thrust into a whirlwind of paralyzing fear. Lt. Col. Dave Grossman coined it "The Human Phobia of Death." Like any of our most extreme phobias; spiders, snakes or heights, our entire being will immediately be galvanized. It will be like getting struck by lightning. Potent chemicals and hormones, like adrenalin and dopamine, will flood our bloodstream. The effects of which will throw your brain into an ultra DEFCON 1 level of security lockdown. From here, only the bodily functions required to perceive the Threat, determine an immediate response and then react to said Threat, will function. Everything else goes on lockdown.

You simply revert back to the Caveman Brain where the only thing that matters is survival. It's at this moment that you will either Fight, Flee or Freeze. Sadly, most freeze, bringing unavoidable death.

2. **Heart Rate Explosion:** An adults normal resting heart rate lives anywhere between (60-80) bpm. Optimal competitive function lives between (115-145) bpm. At this range you're afforded the perfect combination of blood & oxygen flow throughout your body, which enables optimal performance of your entire system. However, for the average citizen who's never faced an actual deadly attack, it's entirely possible for your heart rate to spike between (180-220) bpm or even higher. This is a very dangerous range. Even during normal everyday exercise, like running on a treadmill, if maintained over an extended period of time, this can easily cause cardiac arrest. This range is CATASTROPHIC while in heated battle. Due to the presence of the abnormally high levels of dangerous chemicals, the tidal wave of adrenalin and dopamine; which is violently pumping through you, if your heart rate isn't brought back to a safe level, cardiac arrest can occur within seconds as opposed to minutes. Even if you avoid cardiac arrest, at this range your body teeters between Conditions Gray & Black, meaning you're on the verge of total physical shutdown, like an engine seizing from a lack of oil.

3. **Loss of Peripheral Vision:** This is known as 'Focused Vision' or 'Tunnel Vision'. During attack the ONLY thing you will see is what you need to see. The color of the leaves on a distant tree, the little old lady crossing the street, or even the gigantic skyscraper standing directly behind the person trying to kill you. These are all irrelevant and will likely be completely erased from your perceived vision. This can be a good thing as it will give you a laser beam like, focused type of clarity of your Threat, but what if you're attacked by two or more individuals? Or what about when you consider your response and begin to fire back? Where are your rounds going to go should they miss? Will they hit the little old lady crossing the street? Or the family quietly eating their lunch in the restaurant directly behind your Threat?

4. **Loss of Near Vision:** Think about this, if you can't see your sights because your eyes simply can't see them; due to the fact that your eyes are ONLY trained on that which is trying to actively kill you, how are you going to use your sights to hit your Threat? While under attack, your eyes will see only what they need to see. Because your sights aren't trying to kill you, your eyes won't see them. Again, all your eyes car about is focusing on whomever or whatever it straying to kill you. This sort of phasing out of non-threatening objects is also true for other objects or non-treating people within the spectrum of your near vision.

5. **Loss of Depth Perception:** We rely on our ability to decipher depth in relation to our proximity to objects and surfaces around us. A drastic loss of this important sense would be like trying to fight while experiencing vertigo. Not knowing the true distance to objects in your immediate environment, increases the likelihood that you will trip or stumble, making you completely vulnerable and useless during attack. Understanding this now can help to elevate moments of panic should this occur during your fight.

6. **Auditory Exclusion:** As a result of the perceived likelihood of death, you may experience a temporary loss of hearing. Similar to 'Focused Vision', your ears

will be trained on your Threat and will completely block out the plethora of sounds in your environment. A good example of this is best understood by those who've ever hunting before. When they raise their rifle and shoot their game, the report of the rifle sounds like a muffled pop-gun and their hearing is hardly affected. Yet shooting that same rifle on the range absent hearing protection would leave their ears ringing in pain. Much of this is due to the high levels of adrenaline and dopamine that will surge through your body. In a real gunfight you'll likely experience the same kinds of auditory effects, where everything but your Threat appears muffled.

7. **Loss of Fine Motor Skills:** We rely on Fine Motor Skills for everything. In many ways it's what separates us from primates. Our ability to thread a needle provides the clothing on our backs. Our ability to put thought to paper, by holding a small pen to artistically communicate thoughts and ideas on paper, affords us the ability to expand our understanding. This fine motor skill alone; manipulating a pen to put thoughts on paper, provides blueprints of success for our children and our children's children. Our abilities to finely manipulate our bodies enables us to dominate our environment. However, while under deadly attack, your physiological system is taken out of balance and you will lose the ability to do simple physical things. Under these situations you're left with trying to force a square peg through a round hole or sinking a small nail on a wall with a 20 lb. sledgehammer.

8. **The Slow Motion Effect:** A well known phenomenon, which effects most people who experience extreme high levels of stress during deadly attack, is perceived slow motion. Time itself appears to literally come to a halt and barely ticks by. The best way to articulate this is to compare it to the scene in the movie 'The Matrix' where Neo dodges the torrent of bullets being fired at him, while he bends backwards and manipulates his body here and there, dodging every slow moving bullet slicing through the air. Similarly, time will appear to slow so much so that your movements may appear to be a sort of out-of-body experience.

9. **The Hyper Speed Effect:** Another phenomenon is the sense that your world has just jumped into a hyper speed wormhole. Sometimes people experience a weird mixture of the two where they experience a most bewildering tug-of-war of some outside force randomly pulling them from hyper speed to slow motion and back. A good example of this is seen in the movie 'Contact' when Dr. Ellie Arroway shoots through the Space Time Continuum and is violently torn from one world to the next. At one moment she sits in the harnessed seat of her spherical time machine. Then without warning, she's pulled up and out of the machine, looking down at herself from a God like third person view. For some people, a deadly attack can cause a very similar disturbing state of psychoses.

10. **Tormenting Thoughts:** Another extremely common effect from this type of stress is an onslaught of horribly vulgar and disturbing thoughts. For some they see their life literally pass before their eyes as if they were sitting in a movie theater; eating popcorn, while they quickly reach the climatic and tragic end of their life story. For others it's as crazy as the most exotic acid trip causing insane hallucinations. For instance, during one of my Deadly Force incidents, I swear I saw the suspect's vehicle turn into Magnetron, as it sped

towards me, spilling sparks from its wheels which looked like waves of fire. A buddy of mine later explained to me that during one of his shootings, he saw a little green Leprechaun who continually taunted him throughout the gunfight telling him, "You're gonna dieeee.... You're gonna dieeee..." These kinds of psychotic trips can make it extremely difficult to maintain effective situational awareness and decipher truth from fiction.

11. **Loss of Bowel & Bladder Control:** This is probably something you never thought of when considering how you'll respond to a deadly attack on your life. The reality is our bodies will react absent cognitive thought. At that moment there is only one goal in mind, survival. Average normal bodily functions will go on lockdown, providing ample energy and blood flow for those organs which are needed to provide the essential functions to secure survival. This means if you have a full bladder or are close to passing your last meal, it's entirely possible that you will do so right then and there.

Combat Hydraulics...

Hopefully this chapter underlined the fact that Combat is the most chaotically charged, out of control, consistently fast moving environment known to man. Its hydrostatic qualities are measured in thousandths of seconds multiplied by pounds per square inch. The fluidity of this environment is as volatile as the ocean tide and as random as the ebb and flow of its surge. Sure you might be a competent swimmer in the backyard pool. Hell, you may even be able to hold your breath under water for 5-minutes. Surviving the converging surge in the Straits of Magellan; where the Atlantic and Pacific meet, without a life vest or a wetsuit, that takes a level of proficiency I'd be willing to bet you don't have and Combat is easily as tumultuous as converging oceans.

The act of defending one's self with a firearm is a daunting task even for professionals. However, Combat can be tamed. You may have zero experience and have never actually been in a fight for your life before. You're Caveman Brain my even be pre-wired to Freeze. You may actually be the worst fighter in the entire universe, but don't lose hope. There are ways to pre-condition practical life saving responses and encode them deep within your brain's primitive DOS / C Prompt command. There are things you can do today so you can WIN tomorrow's battle and live to tell about it. It starts here, by preparing your mind for how your body WILL be affected. After this you can develop kinesthetic, Tactical Responses which can be performed in spite of these effects. It's only after you fully understand these scientific realities that you can begin to develop a practical solution that actually works in a real-life gunfight.

My hopes are that this in-depth glimpse into the study of Force Science gives you the knowledge you'll need to develop both a tactical and legal response to Self-Defense. Remember, the vast majority of people haven't a clue about these realities and this includes the Judge, Jury and even your attorney. It's up to you to make this an integral part of your Defense strategy, so you can educate those involved and assure that you're not left being wrongly convicted for something that's completely out of your control.

Chapter 4

Pleading The 5th

As Ol Murphy's Law goes, "If something could go wrong it will go wrong" and that's exactly what happened. However, because you had long past changed your way of thinking and developed a 'What When Mentality', you were ready for the 'Fight' long before you ever met your adversary. It could have been in a parking lot, while walking down a dark alley or you could have even been confronted in your own home. Regardless of the circumstances, your life has just been threatened and you've been forced to defend it and defend it you did. You've just used your handgun in Self-Defense and killed your attacker. Now what???

Hopefully, you've done your due diligence before hand and also prepared an effective *ZuluShield* Proactive Legal Defense. On the diagram on page (7) we determined that a sound Legal Defense Plan was key to ANY use of Self-Defense. Throughout the previous chapters, you've undoubtedly learned just how important a Proactive Legal Defense truly is, and hopefully you've taken the time to follow the 3 Steps to Success and acquired the tools you'll soon need when it comes to determining the justification for your future actions.

Regardless of how well you've prepared or how comprehensive your *ZuluShield* Catalogue might be, there are a few key steps you <u>MUST</u> take directly following any use of Self-Defense. This chapter is dedicated to a process called the *ZuluDefense*. It's a guide on what to do immediately 'After' the use of Self-Defense and it's something nobody teaches. As a former Organized Crime Investigator, I have a very unique understanding of what you <u>NEED</u> to know, to keep you from inadvertently incriminating yourself and ending up behind bars. The process is extremely straight forward and is really more of a check-list of sorts. However, DON'T take this chapter lightly because what you do directly following an incident of this nature, may mean the difference between you walking free or fighting to prove your innocence from a jail cell.

The *ZuluDefense* consists of two main check lists and one companion card; the *ZuluDefense Card*, which is carried with you in our wallet or purse so you always have an easy to follow reference to help you manage such an overwhelmingly stressful experience. Remember, a Criminal Investigation into your actions <u>WILL</u> be initiated within minutes of your use of Self-Defense. This <u>WILL</u> be the most chaotic, out-of-control situation you've likely ever experienced. What you 'Do' and 'Say' directly following the incident, is vital and *ZuluDefense* <u>WILL</u> help you maneuver through the storm.

Before the incident...

Prior to this dreadful day it's important that you've completed the following:

1. Develop a *ZuluShield* Proactive Legal Defense Plan. Make your Legal Defense bulletproof by utilize this system and following it's steps.

2. Follow Step 3 on Page (35). Build your 'Firewall' and retain an attorney experienced with Self-Defense claims. Bring them up to speed on your *ZuluShield* Proactive Legal Defense Plan. Remember to input their information on your *ZuluDefense Card* and like good Ol American Express, "Don't leave home without it!"

3. Find at least two back-up Defense Attorney's in your area. Make sure to keep their information handy in case you're unable to reach your main attorney. While being questioned by police, it doesn't matter if it's a back-up attorney or not, any decent attorney will advise you accordingly, form a buffer and keep you from incriminating yourself. Remember to input their information on your *ZuluDefense Card*.

4. Become a student of 'Self-Defense Law'. Get to know the Federal standards, State and Local statutes and ordinances as well as Case Law.

5. Secure a copy of the *ZuluFight Fight To Win System*. Use our QR Code on Page (284) or visit our website. Learn the Kata of Firearms Self-Defense and why this is the most scientifically proven way to train for a real fight. Discover the dynamics of Firearms Self-Defense and prepare yourself accordingly so you're ready for tomorrow's deadly attack.

6. Seek professional firearms instruction beyond *ZuluFight*. It's vital to learn actual combative tactics. Check out our training opportunities and learn how to play tactical Chess while your Threat's left playing Checkers.

7. Become a student of 'Self-Defense' both armed and unarmed. Maintain an awareness of any articles, books or news events related to the subject. Seek training in practical martial arts forms such as Krav Maga. Learn as much as you can about the subject, as well as real-world incidents where individuals have used Self-Defense.

8. Develop a habit of documentation. Be diligent with ZuluShield. The more data you put in, the greater legal protection you'll have right there at your fingertips tomorrow.

You won the fight, now what?

It's important to remember just how chaotic this event will be. Its crucial you know NOW that you should fully expect to react in any manner of ways and that however you react, is completely normal. The most important thing to keep in mind directly following the incident, is that your battle is <u>NOT</u> over. You need to keep your guard up and be aware. Even though you defeated your attacker, you will soon become the focus of a major investigation. What you do and say from here, will make or break your Legal Defense.

Calling 911...

Obviously someone's going to need to notify police. If someone else is present, ask them to make the call. While they call 911, CALL YOUR ATTORNEY! If no one else is present, call 911. However, you MUST be very careful what you say.

Remember 911 calls are recorded and WILL be used as evidence in the case. The dispatcher will be asking question after question, DO NOT under any circumstances incriminate yourself or admit to your involvement. The ONLY thing the dispatcher needs to know is where police need to respond, that is all. They will want to keep you on the phone, be respectful and tell them you can't. Hang-up then CALL YOUR ATTORNEY!

Again the ONLY information you should give is the address and that you are requesting Police & Medical. They will try their hardest to keep you talking and on the phone and cite 'Officer Safety' concerns. Regardless, your number one priority is to speak with your attorney. So give the dispatcher your location and hang-up.

Many cell phones are placed in a default 'Emergency Call Mode' after dialing 911. In order for you to use your phone after calling 911, you may need to power off you phone and restart it. Other phones may simple give you an option to return to normal function.

Call your attorney!

After you've defeated your attacker and they are no longer a threat to you, your number one priority is getting your attorney on scene as quickly as possible. That means you need to call them immediately. When you speak with your attorney, be VERY mindful if anyone can hear you. Seclude yourself if at all possible and give them the basics. Tell them you used Self-Defense and require them to respond immediately because you are about to be questioned by police. Also request that they contact them Private Investigator and ask that they respond to begin an independent investigation. Follow your attorney's direction to the 'T' and remain silent until they arrive.

Police Interaction...

One of the biggest concepts you must get used to now, is that the police are NOT your friend, when it relates to the investigation of your use of Self-Defense. This is the number one biggest misstep that the vast majority of people get caught-up with. The police are there to investigate a 'Crime' and 'You' are the subject of the alleged offense. Because of this, ANYTHING you do or say WILL be used against you. Your number one goal at this point, is to get your attorney on-scene as quickly as possible and to distance yourself of police as much as possible.

Police officers are experts at getting people to talk. They know they can't legally force you to speak, however their presence alone is intimidating for everybody. The real problem is your mindset. Subconsciously, we tend to view police as the ultimate authority. Because of this, we're extremely susceptible to being tricked into giving statements. It's crucial that you remember that YOU are in control of your destiny. YOU determine what you say and what you don't say, its all up to you NOT them.

Once police become aware of your involvement, they will try and try and try to sneak bits of information out of you. Whatever you do, DON'T give statements whatsoever under ANY circumstances, without direction from your attorney. Again, this will be the MOST stressful and chaotic event of your life, but you MUST remain in control of your 'Speech'.

Be respectful at all times but remember you DO NOT have to answer ANY questions whatsoever, regardless of how big or small the question is. You MUST take advantage of your 5th Amendment protection and refuse to speak without your attorney present. No mater what, DON'T give in. No mater how bad you feel inside or how rude you may think it is, DO NOT tell them ANYTHING about the incident, your involvement, if you were present, how you got there, anything. They don't need to know the details until you've consulted with your attorney. At that point your attorney will advise you on how to respond to their questions.

Remember your freedom depends on your silence. You can not be arrested unless police have Probable Cause to do so. That means they need to know that they're at least 51% certain that you committed a crime. So DON'T help them reach that threshold. Saying you "Shot" the attacker out of "Self-Defense" only helps the police. Unless they can 'Prove' otherwise, they can't arrest you. Even if they have a dead attacker on your living room floor, a firearm which 'Could' have been used, and nobody else present but you, they still don't have Probable Cause that 'You' shot the attacker unless YOU tell them. So DON'T. Instead, be respectful, silent and wait for your attorney.

How to plead the 5th...

The 5th Amendment of the United States Constitution is very, very clear, you DO NOT need to speak whatsoever. So exactly 'What' you say should be guarded and very specific and selective.

When police arrive be respectful and cooperative to a point but NOT to the point that you start giving details about yourself or the incident. Police will question you and they will keep questioning you. There is a way though, that you can stop the questioning dead in its tracks by saying the following:

"I will not give statements of any form whatsoever, without my attorney present. I request that any and all questioning cease until that time. Thank you. May I call my attorney?"

Memorizes this statement verbatim. Each time you're asked a question; any question, recite this statement, then request to call your attorney. If you recite this statement each time and don't give any more information, not even your name, they will have zero to work with. This statement is conveniently printed on the back of our *ZuluDefense Card*, meaning you'll always have it with you.

Combat Breathing...

This incident will effect your physiology to the point that you could pass-out. Even if you haven't reached that point, your ability to think properly will be substantially compromised until you can bring your blood pressure down.

The best way to do this is by practicing what's called 'Combat Breathing'. The process is extremely simple and its completely effective. Following the process will oxygenate your bloodstream with the correct balance of oxygen, while also forcing your heart rate to return to a much more manageable state.

To practice Combat Breathing do the following:

1. Inhale for a count of (4). One-thousand-one, one-thousand-two, one-thousand-three and one-thousand-four.

2. Pause and hold it in for a count of (4). One-thousand-one, one-thousand-two, one-thousand-three and one-thousand-four.

3. Exhale for a count of (4). One-thousand-one, one-thousand-two, one-thousand-three and one-thousand-four.

4. Pause and hold it in for a count of (4). One-thousand-one, one-thousand-two, one-thousand-three and one-thousand-four.

5. Repeat for (5) minutes or until your heart rate returns to a normal state.

Taking back the wheel...

Your life has literally just been thrown into a whirlwind of chaotic furry. However, your battle has only just begun. The sooner you're able to take back the reins, the more successful you'll be in weathering the impending legal storm. What follows are two extremely useful guides on exactly what to do step-by-step the day of the incident and the days, weeks and months to follow. It's essential that you memorize these steps and refer to them as often as possible.

Directly following the incident:

(Refer to your ZuluDefense Card when possible)

1. Move to a position of cover and assess yourself for injuries.

2. Notify 911. If others are present, have them make the call. If not, then you make the call. However, remember to refrain from giving them any details other than your location and that you need police & medical assistance. Then hang up.

3. Now Call your attorney. If you can't get through, call one of your back-up attorneys. Advise them that you've been forced to use Self-Defense and will soon be questioned by police. Make sure you request that they respond immediately. Also request that they have their Private Investigator respond to begin an independent investigation.

4. Assess the scene and take mental notes but DO NOT tamper with any evidence. Try and memorize the layout and how things appear as well as who else is present and what vantage point they may have had.

5. Be respectful when police arrive. When they ask the first question tell them: "I will not be giving statements of any form whatsoever, without my attorney present. I request that any and all questioning cease until my attorney is present. Thank you. May I call my attorney?" Then remain silent and DO NOT give statements whatsoever under any circumstances without your attorney present.

6. Practice Combat Breathing: In for (4) count, hold for (4) count, exhale for (4) count, pause for (4) count and repeat until your heart rate returns to a normal state.

24-hours and beyond, until you've been completely cleared

1. Stress plays a major role directly following an incident of this magnitude. You will unavoidably experience both physiological and psychological effects, which will likely have a substantial effect on your daily life. For this reason, it is crucially important that you immediately see both your practitioner and a licensed mental health specialist. Don't be ashamed or afraid. Even if you think you don't need to see anyone, you DO. Remember, your innocence will rely on how well you're capable of weathering this storm. So the healthier you can be, the more likely you are to have a successful outcome.

2. It is imperative that you eat, hydrate and sleep as normal as possible. You WILL find this difficult to balance in the first few days to weeks, but the sooner you can bring these three areas back into rhythm, the sooner you'll be capable of having the mental and psychological clarity to aid in your Defense. If you find it too difficult to manage, seek medical help.

3. In the first 24-48 hours, your physiological state of being is greatly compromised. For this reason, it is IMPERATIVE that you refrain from giving ANY formal statements whatsoever even with your attorney present within the fist 24-48 hours. Even if your attorney say's its safe to do so, I would suggest you have them first consult with me, I'd gladly convince them just how dangerous a move that is. Sciences is clear that following an incident of this magnitude, you will be philologically incapable of remembering vital information nor will your brain have the clarity to formulate solid thought to assist in articulating the facts with any degree of accuracy. So DON'T!

4. As soon as possible utilize the 'Notes Log' section of *ZuluShield* and take personal notes of the incident. Be as descriptive as possible. Jot down ANYTHING even if it's just bits and pieces.

5. It's a good idea to keep a pocket audio recorder with you at all times. This way you can make voice memos which can be dictated at a later date. Over the days and months following the incident, your memory will sporadically return, often times at random times. You could be tying your shoes, walking to your car, at work or at the store. Wherever you are, stop and document your thought so you don't forget it.

6. Resist ALL urges to speak with the others about the incident. This includes your family. Follow this golden rule through the entirety of all legal proceedings. It will be difficult especially with family, but it is the BEST way of protecting your attorney's Defense strategy.

7. It is a good select and involve a competent Civil Defense Attorney as soon as entirely possible even though you have not yet been formally sued. Infusing your Civil Defense Attorney at such an early stage is HUGE! Doing so gives them a first-hand view of your entire Criminal battle as well as ample time to strategize the most solid Civil Defense. It also assures important elements of this Defense don't get lost in translation over the span of time from when your Criminal Defense is first initiated, to when Civil Action is eventually brought against you. Make sure they are on-board with your Criminal Defense Attorney's team so they do not hamper your Criminal Legal Defense in any way.

8. Under NO circumstances should you EVER speak with the media about the incident until you've been completely cleared both Criminally and Civilly.

9. Plan for a VERY lengthy, costly and extraordinarily stressful ordeal. This will likely last a year or even longer after the incident. Stay confident, healthy and always be aware that you're likely being surveilled by police, which may include your texts, phone and other forms of private communication. It might also be wise to suspend your social media accounts altogether.

10. Prior to ANY Criminal or Civil proceeding and as soon after the incident as possible, instruct your attorney to contact me. My experience as both an expert in Use-of-Force, Firearms and Tactics, but also as an Organized Crime Investigator, will greatly assist your Legal Defense team in developing the best Legal Defense possible.

11. Above all, if you are innocent, <u>DON'T MAKE PLEA DEALS</u>!!! If your attorney's can't effectively defend you, hire a new one. Always have a second and third attorney on stand-by and <u>NEVER</u> admit to wrongdoing if you're innocent. Even if it means jail time, your ability to effectively appeal a wrongful conviction is greatly compromised and often times impossible to overturn if you agree to a Plea Deal. So <u>DON'T DO IT</u>!

ZuluDefense Card...

No mater how well you prepare for the chaos of an event of this magnitude, you will still be overwhelmed. Most people, especially those who have never actually had to fight for their lives, go into a state of semi-shock directly following incidents like this. Regardless of your degree of shock, you will experience the distractions of stress to one degree or another.

A 'Distracted' mind is the LAST thing you want to rely on when police arrive to begin their investigation. Trying to think back about the steps you must take directly following the use of Self-Defense, while also being distracted by the overwhelming torrent of emotions of the incident itself, is a daunting task at best. The consequences of doing the wrong thing during the initial phase of the investigation, is far too great for you to chance. For this reason, I've designed a very handy card which can be carried in your wallet or purse at all times. No bigger than a business card, the *ZuluDefense Card* gives you a step-by-step guide of exactly what to do immediately following the incident. It even has the previous mentioned 'I Will Not Speak' statement printed on it, which means even under stress, you'll be able to recite this all important statement to police and protect yourself from being tricked into talking.

Another ingenious aspect of the *ZuluDefense Card* is the Attorney Contact section located on the back. This gives you (3) fill in the black places to document the names and phone number of your main attorney and two other back-up attorney's should you fail to reach yours. This is HUGE as it automatically makes this card a 'Privileged Document'. This means that if for any reason you are arrested, the information on this card can NOT be concealed from you. That means that while your other personal items may be confiscated at booking, they MUST either allow you to keep the card on your person or provide another means for you to retain this information as it pertains to your Legal Defense.

With the *ZuluDefense Card*, you'll always be prepared for what happens next, no matter how stressed or scatterbrained you are immediately following the most chaotic event of your life. Don't Leave Home Without It!

Don't Leave Home Without It

www.zulutactical.com/zuludefense

Chapter 5

ZuluProofing

When it comes to Self-Defense claims, your attorney plays an extremely critical role. As mentioned previously, Self-Defense claims in and of themselves, are the most difficult kinds of cases for attorneys to present in Court, especially those resulting in the death of an attacker. Even those situations, which may appear to be cut-and-dry and unmistakably justified; as it pertains to the 'Criminality' of your actions, could easily be looked at very differently, once the case hits a Civil Court. Due to a completely unbalanced Justice System, totally innocent 'Victims' of a heinous deadly attacks, are regularly found Civilly Liable during Civil Court Proceedings, meaning the victim is left paying-out millions of dollars in civil penalties. *ZuluShield* was specifically designed to protect victims from both the Criminal and Civil whirlwind which directly follows any use of Self-Defense.

In Chapter (1) we discussed two overriding differences between Criminal and Civil Court proceedings. While its true there are many differences, the Burden of Proof and who's shoulders said 'Burden' lies, are the most significant variances, which threaten ANY Self-Defense claim. The sad reality is that the only thing an attacker's family has to do; Civilly, is convince the Judge that there's a 51% 'Chance' that you were simply 'Negligent' in your choice of action. They DON'T even have to prove malice or ill-intent.

Let's revisit the Home Invasion scenario from Chapter (1), where you've been startled in the middle of the night, to someone breaking into your home. Fearing for the safety of both yourself and your family, you decided to arm yourself and go about doing a Safety Clear of your Home.

Now if you remember, you decided to take matters in your own hands because you know that in all reality, police are too far away to intercede. You fear for the safety of yourself and your family and you're not going to hide in wait, while someone harms your loved ones.

During the process of your Safety Clear, you've happened upon the assailant, whom you're surprised to see standing just 15-feet from you, in the middle of your living room. You quickly noticed him starting to approach you. You can't see his hands, much less make out his face. However, you know that 'Time' is NOT on your side and so, you decide to shoot. As it turns out, the assailant was killed and was found to be completely unarmed. In this scenario where you Reasonably Justified in the use of Deadly Force, or not?

As we've discussed, Criminally you should be fine. Not only do most police officers understand the immediate risk the assailant posed to you, but the 'Burden' to prove you committed unlawful homicide; under these circumstances, is far too high in Criminal Court. What would likely happen is the police would perform a full fledged Homicide Investigation, forward their findings to the District Attorney, who would then determine your actions were clearly in Self-Defense. That is as long as you didn't say, "I thought he was going to steal my TV." Again, you're protecting 'Life' not mere property.

How about Civilly? What would the outcome be if this very same scenario was brought before a Civil Court? Not good, not good at all. That is without a ton's more 'Reason' as to why you killed an unarmed man, especially without actually warning him first. Oh and that 'Reason' needs to come in the form of tangible proof, as to why it's 'Reasonable' for you to have assumed you were in immediate danger of losing your life. This 'Tangible' proof, needs to clearly show why another reasonable person would have made the very same decision as you did, if presented with the same set of circumstances.

Remember, in many Civil proceedings, the 'Burden' to prove, rests solely on the shoulders of the accused. This means, you need to present the most solid Legal Defense possible, geared at convincing a naysaying skeptic, that your actions were completely reasonable. In a Civil case, 'You' and only you can prove this, meaning you need to have a surplus of real-world examples already on hand, which clearly show other people defending themselves similarly, under similar circumstances. This Chapter focuses on the process of capturing this vital information and the steps you must take to adequately insolate yourself form both Criminal and Civil Court proceedings.

The Reverse-RICO...

In 2015, a Connecticut woman sued her cousin due to an "aggressive hug" which resulted in the woman sustaining injury. Apparently, the cousin's young son, ran up to the woman, threw his arms around her legs and hugged her out of extreme excitement upon seeing the woman. Unfortunately, the woman fell backwards landing on her wrist, fracturing it in multiple locations. What resulted were extremely expansive medical bills to which the woman was advised by her attorney, to sue the cousin's Home Insurer, for $127,000.

Everyday homeowners are successfully sued, resulting in substantial Civil pay-outs, all for unavoidable accidents, which occur on their property. If an innocent homeowner can be successfully sued for NOT doing anything wrong, how much more likely do you suppose a homeowner could be sued for 'Intentionally' causing the death of another on their property, even if that death was the result of Self-Defense? In all reality, if you cause the death or injury to someone else; even in Self-Defense, you most certainly will be sued. Unless you present a solid Defense, you could be left with legal penalties, which can easily reach into the millions of dollars.

The reason why it's so common for innocent people being found 'Liable' in Civil Court, is in my opinion largely due to a wrong approach by their attorney's. Think about it, if 'Innocent' people are regularly being found Liable for things completely out of their control, then something's obviously very wrong. What most people do is blame it on the Justice System and consider Civil lawsuits to be unbeatable and concede, which is precisely why most Civil cases end in a settlement prior to Trial.

While I do believe the Justice System is completely unbalanced and totally unfair 'Civilly', it is the system we have so the longer we complain about it, the more innocent people end up with the short end of the stick. I believe a lot of this is a result of poor legal guidance on the part of the attorney. Too often Civil Law attorneys opt for a quick compromise because of a lack of confidence that they'll be able to present a winning case in Court.

Let's translate this. What's happing is that the vast majority of legal professionals in this country, who make a minimum of $300 per-hour and who have been schooled at some of the most prestigious educational programs, are incapable at actually defending innocent victims. That is completely unacceptable. The reason for this failure is due to the wrong 'Approach'. The reality is that attorneys have failed to develop wining strategies to overcome the hurdles presented in Civil proceedings.

When I began instructing individuals in Self-Defense and Tactics, I was immediately appalled by the reality that sometimes, completely innocent victims actually end up losing everything, just because they determined to defend themselves as apposed to being helplessly murdered. For years I shook my head like most other instructors, with a feeling of complete frustration and with no real solution to offer my students. That was until my time as RICO Investigator. It wasn't until then that I realized just how bulletproof a 'Revers-RICO' could actually be, especially during a Civil proceeding. Remember, it's the horribly lower Burden of Proof, combined with the daunting predicament Civil Defendants face, where they're forced to prove their own innocence as apposed to the Plaintiff proving guilt, which makes a Civil proceeding the most dangerous threat to ANYONE who's forced to use Self-Defense.

For fifty years our most successfully capable Federal Prosecutors approached 'Organized Crime' with the very same unsatisfactory approach, due to a complete lack of 'Strategy'. From the 1920's to the 1970's, our nation was plagued by Organized Crime groups such as la Costa Nostra and other mafia organizations. Essentially these entities had organized themselves so perfectly, that they easily and almost entirely skirted past all our laws, while remaining completely unchecked for the most part. For years our most experienced prosecutors failed to secure solid Criminal convictions against this country's most dangerous and notorious individuals. That was until 1970 when the US Attorney's Office determined the failure rested on their own shoulders. They had finally realized that they had been approaching Organized Crime with the wrong mindset.

The result was the enactment of the Racketeer Influenced and Corrupt Organizations Act (RICO). Prosecutors had finally developed a bulletproof strategy for attacking this cancer and since 1970, they've been extremely successful in substantially decreasing the ability for these groups to operate unhindered.

What prosecutors learned, was that unless they could trip-up a defendant on Tax Invasion charges, it was extremely unlikely they'd be able to prove wrongdoing because the Burden of Proof Criminally, was far to high. The reality was that, even though Prosecutors knew an individual had committed murder and had physical evidence to support that claim, most Organized Crime 'Individuals' where far too insulated by their Organization. This made it extremely difficult to definitively prove their case in the long run, much less impact the overall organization as a whole. So what they did was develop an in-depth multi-faceted approach and attacked the 'Organization' as apposed to the 'Individual', making RICO cases the most difficult case to defend against.

The genius behind a RICO Case has to do with its complexity of strategy, or in other words its breath. For instance, in your typical Murder trial, the Prosecution's case is narrow and completely limited to the evidence found and how that particular evidence relates to the accused individual. Unless an accomplice played an active roll in the act of murder, the Prosecution in a typical Murder trial is limited to trying an 'Individual' not a group. However, a RICO Murder is vastly different. In this type of case, the Prosecution is afforded a very broad brush approach. Through strategy, investigators use a drag-net method and gather any and ALL information on EVERYONE associated with their suspected killers, to include known associates, current and past business partners, friends and even family members. When I say everything, I mean everything. The goal is to find a common link between the suspects, their family, friends and associates, in multiple ways so as to create a 'Nexus' of corporate corporation amongst the 'Group', that's so airtight that each and every individual tied to the actual accused killer, becomes an 'Active Participant' in the murder itself, due solely to their combined proximity to one another. As apposed to proving an 'Individual' committed murder, with RICO you prove the 'Enterprise' committed the murder and end-up convicting the lot. While this process is much more intensive, requiring more organization, planning and time, RICO cases are nearly impossible to beat.

By reversing this concept into a 'Defense Strategy' as apposed to a Prosecutory Method, a 'Victim' of say a Wrongful Death Civil lawsuit, who used 'Criminally Justified Self-Defense' thereby killing a completely 'Unarmed' Home Invasion assailant, is afforded a kind of impenetrable force shield of Civil protection, that if used properly, is almost completely unbeatable. Through reverse engineering RICO, for a practical Self-Defense legal strategy, the 'Victim' is now provided a multi-faceted drag-net of Civil alibis, capable of nullifying even the most strategic arguments a Plaintiff could possibly present. This approach gives you the capability of preempting the Plaintiff's claims, by collecting years and years of preselected and individually strategized examples of 'Reason' with enough factual density to disprove each of the Plaintiff's individual claims, while also proving that any foreseeable method of Self-Defense under any manner of circumstances, are not only acceptable, reasonable and justified but are backed by a kaleidoscope of individual avenues to counter EACH particular argument a Plaintiff may allege.

Having ten or fifteen different examples of why other reasonable people used the same Self-Defense Response as you, under similar circumstances, then combining that with a dozen or so scientific facts as well as statistical data as to why your Use-of-Force was not only reasonable but also 'Essential' under the circumstances presented, means the Plaintiff is primitively denied an unhindered passage, is immediately placed on the backs of their heels and is left with a Reactionary Legal Strategy. In turn, they're forced to attempt a Mt. Everest summit, without equipment or even supplies. Since you've spent years picking apart their future claim, they'll be left spending years scratching their heads. With *ZuluShield*, when a future Prosecutor or Plaintiff presents a particular argument, your attorney is afforded dozens of ways to rebut those claims entirely.

A calculative approach...

To give your Legal Defense the best probability of withstanding even the most extreme attack, you must be 'Calculative' in your approach to it's design. When an architect builds a structure, they put 'Thought' into its shape and definition, its composition, its reinforcement, its set-up and to what it's actually established upon. By far, the MOST critical structural component is its foundation.

The best way to infuse structural integrity into any Legal Defense is by building said defense on a solid foundation. The kind of legal foundation you require is one that's been reinforced much like a Forman uses rebar and steel beams to provide a skyscraper its integrity. ZuluShield provides your Future Legal Defense the strongest foundation, reinforced to give you the most secure option for tomorrow's battle.

Here's the methodology to our calculative approach to tomorrow's legal battle:

1. **Proactive:** The whole concept is tethered to a proactive What When Mindset with a proactive fact finding habit of seeking, digesting and retaining, preselected forms of information, which in turn become a pixel which gives contrast and definition to the overall picture you'll one-day paint in Court, as you overwhelmingly prove your case.

2. **Multifaceted:** When you need one fish, you use a fishing pole but if you're in the business of fish, you use a net. The wider it's span, the greater catch potential your net has. *ZuluShield* attacks tomorrow's legal battle by taking a broad brush approach to the types of information one gathers. This way you're sure to have a surplus, affording you multiple counters to any particular accusation.

3. **Comprehensive:** What's inside an object determines its mass. The more massive a given object's density is, the more gravity it has, making it a much more difficult object to budge. Having (10) individual ways to prove (1) theory, gives the opposition the impression that your defense is so well orchestrated, that you're likely to present countless more undefeatable obstacles to their cause, leaving them to strongly consider pulling their claim altogether.

4. **Organized:** One of the reasons *ZuluShield* is so successful is in how well its information is organized. The manner by which it retains critical bits of data for future use, makes maneuvering through its data sources an extremely easy and straightforward task. When it comes time for your attorney to go about selecting important information needed to support your Defense, they'll quickly be able to find exactly what they want, while also maintaining the ability to assess and see what other potential sources of support are available. To support a particular argument.

The pillars, from left to right, are labeled: Purposed, Honest, Balanced, Consistent, Complete. The base steps read: The Firewall / Attorney Communiqué / What When Mentality.

5 Pillars for a successful strategy...

The whole intent behind adopting a *ZuluShield* approach to Self-Defense, is that you fully expect favorable results in the long-run. What you're hedging on is an expectation that you'll have the capability of overcoming future legal hurtles, through the use of strategically documented evidence, so as to support said Defense. The key word here is 'Strategy', but what makes Strategy, strategic.

In order to turn a 'Good Plan' into a Strategically Good plan', you must be serious and calculative with each step. By placing an emphasis on 'Excellence', you automatically increase the quality of the raw product. In terms of the quality of ZuluProofing one commits themselves to, it boils down to how well they adhere to (5) important Pillars of Strategy. The more well founded your commitment to excellence is in these (5) areas, the greater density your overall Legal Defense actually has. The denser your Legal Defense becomes, the more 'Weight' it retains when your future use of Self-Defense is weighed in Court.

5. **Purposed:** With out purpose your plan has no purpose. Giving your plan purpose, brings it alive. The concept here is to give your plan direction, where by the implementation of your plan, strategically align it so that it's trajectory brings you to a place of advantage.

6. **Honest:** Honesty lets you know where you're at, where you've been and where you're headed. If you're not honest then there is no possible way to measure your progression or the quality of your efforts.

7. **Balanced:** A balanced approach gives your plan stability. Making it 'Strategically Balanced' means that you've calculated your steps so as to have a built in gyroscopic counter weight, so that no mater where you end up or by what angle your plan is attacked, you're able to maintain 'Level' alignment, assuring you the most favorable ability to achieve a 'Win' in Court. Being strategic here means that you're not too top-heavy or too weak in one area over another.

8. **Consistent:** A consistent approach means that at every step along the way, you're always afforded the same high standard of quality and potential. Consistency also creates important redundancies of structure, making your plan clear and easily understood, regardless of one's point-of-view.

9. **Complete:** To an untrained eye, an unpolished raw diamond could easily be mistaken for an agate and tossed aside. Completeness gives your plan a

polished appearance of quality, which in turn speaks to your character. It also assures there's no loose ends, which could inadvertently be misunderstood or viewed in a negative light.

ZuluShield Components...

This system is broken up into (4) main components:

1. The Chapter Book
2. The Reload
3. The Archive
4. Zdrive (digital version of the Archive)

The Chapter Book is the book you happen to be reading from now. It's divided into (2) sections; the Chapter section and the Logbook Section. The Chapters describe the process as well as communicate important facts and information you'll need to get started on the right foot. The Logbook Section represents the backbone of *ZuluShield*. You'll utilize the logs to document important information and facts you'll use to communicate with your attorney and develop a bulletproof Firearms Legal Defense.

When you run out of available logs, its time to purchase a *Reload*. The *Reload* is basically the main ZuluShield Logbook Section on steroids without chapters. Due to the sheer amount of logs available, the average person should only require one *Reload* per year.

The *Archive* is how you go about capturing all the hard evidence you'll need should you end up in Court. Its where you file and retain physical copies of things like certificates, articles, reports, notes and even digital files, which you've saved on your *Zdrive*. Let's say you compose some notes on a particular topic or incident or maybe a thought, which you believe will play into your Legal Defense. You simply turn to the 'Notes Section' of your *Archive* and file that document in the next available sleeve. Whether you download our *ZuluShield DIY Archive Kit* or purchase your complete *ZuluShield Archive* from our store, you'll always have what you want, when you need it. Simply turn to our handy *ZuluShield* QR Code on Page (284) or visit *www.zulutactical.com/zulushield* to find your *ZuluShield Archive* or kit.

The *Zdrive* is specifically designed for retaining all your digital files. You'll notice the *Zdrive* comes pre-loaded with a sophisticated file hierarchy. This file organization system is essentially a digital version of your *ZuluShield Archive*. You'll also find easy to use report templates, making the process of composing notes and reports, straightforward and easy to do. Should you choose to use your own method of digital file storage, its highly suggested you download our *ZuluShield Zdrive Hierarchy*. This can then be download on to your personal computer or thumb-drive. Simply turn to our handy *ZuluShield* QR Code on Page (284) or visit *www.zulutactical.com/zulushield* to find your *ZuluShield Zdrive Hierarchy* for only $3.99.

Component Retention...

Over the years you're likely to accumulate a number of *ZuluShield Reloads* and may even require a second *Archive.* It's extremely important to remember that the reason you're utilizing this system, is because you're proactively preparing for tomorrow's legal battle. But when, when will tomorrow come? Well if you had a crystal ball and could predict when you'll need this data, you'd probably be better off just predicting when you'd need to use Self-Defense and avoid that situation altogether. Since you're not psychic, you'll have to do what the rest of us do and file your Reloads away. While the IRS can audit you for 7 years. However, *ZuluShield* data is critical to your overall Legal Defense and 'Tomorrow' might not come for several years or even a decade or more. This means you need to make sure to retain ALL your *ZuluShield* products indefinitely. It's even more advisable that you dedicate a safe place and store these items together so as not to misplace them. Whatever you do, guard them with the utmost care because when that day comes and you actually need this information, you'll need it yesterday.

Mightier than the pen...

While this may appear trivial, its not. You should treat your *ZuluShield* log entries as 'Documentary Evidence'. Meaning, you should fully expect each individual, original entry, to be viewed in Court by the Judge and Jury. With this in mind, its extremely important that your entries have a professional appearance to them, that they're neat, easy to read and have Court appropriate language. Its highly suggested that you refrain from using pens and opt for a dependable mechanical pencil. Mechanical pencils are inexpensive, more reliable, neater, mistake proof and capable of extremely fine writing to allow for adequate space within a particular log entry data field.

ZuluProofing...

So how exactly does *ZuluShield* work? It's really quite simple, *ZuluShield* is a 'Mindset', it's about how you view the likelihood of an attack and how you prepare for that likelihood. *ZuluProofing;* the process of implementing the mindset into a 'Lifestyle', placing emphasize on proactively defending future use of Self-Defense, through calculative documentation, is how you 'Strategize'.

ZuluShield is really as easy as 1,2,3. Back in Chapter (2), we discussed the '3 Steps to Success'. If you remember Step (1) had to do with changing your mentality from a 'What If Mindset' to a 'What When Mentality' or What' will you do WHEN someone confronts you with a knife as you walk out your front door in the morning? This is the bedrock of the *ZuluShield* Mindset, it's not a matter of 'If' you'll be attacked but WHEN, and you've committed to preparing for this likelihood, tactically, mentally and legally. The process of documenting this preparation, is meaningless without first acquiring a solid What When Mentality.

Step (2) had to deal with your legal preparation and introduced you to the concept of the 'Attorney Communiqué'. Basically, you've determined that its not 'If' but WHEN you'll be attacked and you've already determined that you will defend yourself. Because of this likelihood, you've determined two things:

1. You'll be focusing on preparing both mentally and physically for this likelihood and will strive to develop the most solid, realistic and practical Self-Defense Responses not only capable of overcoming your foe but which are also completely founded on the Legal Reasonableness Standard.

2. You've decided to initiate a method of communicating your strategy to your attorney so you can acquire both a solid understanding of the laws associated with Self-Defense but also a mechanism of obtaining the very best, most strategic legal advice and services possible, for your future use of Self-Defense.

Step (3) if you remember was 'The Firewall'. Its where you formally initiate contact with a preselected Defense Attorney and where you insulate your Legal Defense, tomorrow by retaining their services today. Step 3 is essential and something you must NOT overlook. Steps (1) and (2) are the steps you will use to begin *ZuluProofing* tomorrow's Legal Defense.

ZuluProofing is where the rubber meets the road in terms of your mental and physical preparation. Through training, you develop realistic responses to any manner of probable threats. With research you go about studying real-world incidents of Self-Defense so as to better determine which responses have the highest probability of success both physically and legally. By brainstorming other likely Self-Defense scenarios; you may someday be faced with, you add the appropriate density required to legitimize your overall approach because it shows just how dedicated you are to the 'Responsibility' of responding appropriately.

This is also where the pencil meets the paper and how you'll go about *ZuluProofing* tomorrow's Legal Defense, through strategically organizing and documenting your training and research. This way, you'll have equipped yourself with dozens upon dozens of different ways to turn your Legal Defense, into individually relevant bite-size bits of factual evidence. Then when tomorrow comes, you'll use it to support the reasoning behind your future use of Self-Defense. *ZuluProofing* is how you go about painting the picture, by identifying and documenting individual examples or 'Pixels' of data you'll use assure it's most clear HD image possible and is capable of easily communicating your 'Reasoning', so that no matter who views this picture or where they view it from, that even a sceptic is fully convinced that your use of Self-Defense wasn't only reasonable but completely and fully expected under the circumstances, which you were faced with at that exact moment.

ZuluShield Logs...

The following sub-sections provide a break-down of *ZuluShield* logs and procedures to better describe them, their function and their intent. It's crucial that you study each section thoroughly so you're completely certain you understand how each log is intended to be used. This way you're *ZuluProofing* with purpose.

As mentioned previously, *ZuluShield* logs represent the backbone to this system. You'll utilize logs to document important data about individual training events, licenses and certificates held, literary facts such as news articles related to Firearms Self-Defense or Use-of-Force, personal notes and contact information. So whether you participated in a high speed, run and gun firearms training course, a *ZuluFight* session at home, read an interesting article about a real-world incident or read a book which relates to Self-Defense or Firearms, *ZuluShield* will asset in translating this vital information into a bulletproof Firearms Legal Defense.

Not only will these log entries form a breadcrumb-trail of your training and knowledge about the subject of Self-Defense, but when it comes time to recall specific facts about your training history or a particular piece of evidence which supports your use of Self-Defense, faithful log entries will make finding this information as easy as turning a page.

Its important to know that *ZuluShield* logs were specifically designed for multiple uses. For instance, the 'Training Log' has data fields for instructor information and course fees. If you're documenting a different type of training such as a *ZuluFight* session or another informal type training, simply place an "N/A" in the field; which doesn't apply, then move on to the next. The concept here is that you'll fill in only the data fields which are applicable to the information you're documenting. Whatever you do, stay consistent. Consistency in documentation is just as important as consistency with your weapon. Don't leave data fields blank and follow the same documentation technique each and every time you make a log entry.

The Legal Notice:

On Page (1) you will find a legal noticed titled 'ATTENTION!!!' You'll find these notices on the front page of every *ZuluShield* product. It's imperative you read this notice in it's entirety, sign and then print your legal name at the bottom of the notice. The intention of this notice is to notify law enforcement officers, that the material and information associated with this system is 'Protected Matter' which can not be destroyed, reviewed, copied or even seized without your authorization. Make sure you take the time to read this section.

Cover Page:

On the bottom of Page (3) you'll find a log intended to be used for inputting your personal information. It is critical that you DON'T skip or overlook this log. Filling out this information will marry this particular *ZuluShield* product to you, making it your own personal Attorney Communiqué. Remember *ZuluShield* isn't just words on paper, it's the foundation of tomorrow's Legal Defense and needs to be yours and yours alone in-order for it to qualify as 'Protected Communication'.

Licenses Logs:

The primary function of this section is to provide both a quick reference checklist of all the licenses you may hold. You are encouraged to think outside the box. Licenses not generally associated with 'Firearms' can actually be VERY useful when you're attempting to present yourself as an everyday law abiding citizen. Professional licenses are also great, in that they showcasing your professional dedication and qualm any fears that you're just some yahoo with a gun. Obviously any licenses related to firearms use and tactics, reflect a person's maturity and perspective when it relates to the level of commitment and responsibility they've taken as prudent firearms owners.

Here is a breakdown of the Licenses Logs:

1. **The 'Concealed Carry List':** Unfortunately, many law abiding citizens have found them selves in VERY hot water for unemotionally carrying their firearms in a State which doesn't recognize their particular CCW License. If you're a CCW License holder, this is an extraordinarily quick and handy way to know exactly which States your CCW license authorizes you to carry in other States. If you are, it's highly suggested you take the time to research which States recognize your CCW license before you travel. Keep in mind, some so-called 'Reciprocity States' may indeed accept your particular CCW license, however they may also require you to apply and obtain their State's license prior to you actually carrying in their State. Usacary.com is a great resource on this matter. Take some time so you're not left guessing. Be sure to keep this log up-to-date as some States tend to change their CCW laws from time to time.

2. **The 'Open Carry List':** If you ever see yourself traveling from your State with your firearm, its probably a good idea to know the rules in those States you'll be passing through. Similar to our 'Concealed Carry List' this log helps you quickly determine which States allow 'Open Carry'. Determining which States participate in 'Open Carry' is pretty simply with the advent of Google. However, keep in mind that although a 'State' may authorize this form of carry, some cities and municipals within that State may not. So do your homework before you travel, refer to this log whenever you're planning a trip and be sure to update the log as laws do change from State to State.

3. **The 'Assault Weapons List':** Here's a great way to quickly know exactly which States allow 'Assault Weapons'. This information is critical for anyone who owns an Assault Weapon and plans to travel with it. Unfortunately, Assault Weapons are over scrutinized hated tools of defense. Inadvertently bringing one into a State that's banned them, will get you in a world of pain should you get caught. Determining which States allow Assault Weapons and Full-Autos, is pretty simply with the advent of Google. However, keep in mind that although a 'State' may actually authorize these types of weapons, some cities and municipals within that State may not. So do your homework before you travel, refer to this log whenever you're planning a trip and be sure to update the log as laws do change from State to State.

4. **The 'Unrestricted Magazines List':** This is a fast and easy way to know exactly which States allow unhindered use of standard and extended firearms magazines of 10 rounds or more. Determining which States allow Unrestricted Magazines, is pretty simply with the advent of Google. However, keep in mind that although a 'State' may actually authorize these types of magazines, some cities and municipals within that State may not. So do your homework before you travel, refer to

this log whenever you're planning a trip and be sure to update the log as laws do change from State to State.

5. **The 'Licenses Log':** This is where you input and retain information about exactly which licenses you hold. If a particular data field doesn't pertain, simply put an simply put an "N/A" in the field; which doesn't apply, then move on to the next. It's highly suggested you retain the original or a physical copy of this license, which can easily be stored in your *ZuluShield* Archive.

Certificates Logs:

The primary function of this section is to provide both a quick reference checklist of all the certifications you may hold. You are encouraged to think outside the box, certifications not generally associated with 'Firearms' can actually be VERY useful when you're attempting to present yourself as an everyday law abiding citizen. Professional certifications are also great, in that they showcasing your professional dedication and qualm any fears that you're just some yahoo with a gun. Obviously any certificates related to firearms use and tactics, reflect a person's maturity and perspective when it relates to the level of commitment and responsibility they've taken as prudent firearms owners.

Training Logs:

The primary function of this section is to provide a detailed overview of your actual training in its chronology, as it relates to Firearms, Tactics, Use of Force, Self-Defense or similar topics. This includes typical firearms classes, private individual training at a firearms range, *ZuluFight* dry-fire training or similar, use-of-force and defensive tactics / martial arts, or any other form of dedicated training.

Individual Training Logs are formatted to allow them to be utilized in many different ways. Think outside the box. If a particular data field is not applicable with your entry, simply put an "N/A" in the field; which doesn't apply, then move on to the next.

There are times when you'll want to write a short report or notes about a particular training session. Remember the objective is to document important facts which may impact tomorrow's Legal Defense. So don't be shy, make notes. Trying to remember important facts later, may be impossible. Be sure to capture important facts about a particular training session. It's vital to document and retain this information 'Today' because they'll likely be critical tomorrow. You might prefer to make a digital copy of your notes via PDF or scanner. Either way you'll want to indicate this in the 'Summery Section' of the Training Log, then retain this file in the 'Training Section' of your *ZuluShield Archive* or *Zdrive*.

Literary Logs:

The primary function of this section is to provide both a detailed catalogue and quick reference of particular literary items you believe to be vital to your Legal Defense. For the most part this section will consist of individual real-world

Self-Defense incidents, use of firearms, Home Invasions, assaults, deadly attacks and the like. This section is also great for documenting literature which describes particular facts relating to Deadly Encounters, crime or anything else you feel is vital for your Defense. This could also be a place where you document a book or editorial which bares precedence on your stance on Self-Defense or firearms use. Remember this section is for documenting real-world incidents and facts as well as any other material, studies or information you've acquired via literary sources.

This information will make a HUGE difference when it comes time to strategize your Legal Defense with your attorney. Being able to hand over specific real-world incidents, studies or editorials, which can be used as actual 'Evidence' to support your actions, will allow for a bulletproof Defense. In a Civil trial; where you'll face a Wrongful Death lawsuit, this section will give you plenty of real-world incidents to prove exactly why your Use of Force was not only justified but more than reasonable and completely supported with real-world facts.

- When documenting an article or news event, its suggested that you print a copy or photocopy the article making sure to retain exactly where it's sourced such as the URL. You might prefer to make a digital copy of this document via PDF or scanner. Either way you'll want to indicate this in the 'Summery Section' of the Literary Log, then retain this file in the 'Literary Section' of our *ZuluShield Archive* or *Zdrive*.

- When documenting a book or more in-depth study, its advisable that you compose a book report. You might prefer to make a digital copy of your report via PDF or scanner. Either way you'll want to indicate this in the 'Summery Section' of the Literary Log, then retain this report in the 'Literary Section' of your *ZuluShield Archive* or *Zdrive*

Multi-Media Logs:

The primary function of this section is to provide both a detailed catalogue and quick reference of multi-media based data you believe to be vital to your legal defense. For the most part this section will consist of capturing audio-video evidence such as YouTube videos, audio-video news stories, recordings and other similar data sources.

This data will make a HUGE difference when it comes time to strategize your Legal Defense with your attorney. Being able to hand over specific real-world incidents which can be used as actual 'Evidence' to support your claim of Self-Defense, will allow for a bulletproof Defense. In a Civil trial; where you'll face a Wrongful Death lawsuit, you'll have plenty of real-world incidents, like the ability to play the 'Nanny Cam Home Invasion' to prove exactly why your Use of Force was not only justified but was also completely reasonable and completely supported by real-world facts.

Notes Logs:

The primary function of this section is to provide a detailed catalogue of any notes or reports you compose pertaining to information you believe to be vital to your Legal Defense. Notes are HUGE. You may think you'll remember all the facts and thoughts you had on a particular issue, but you won't. If you end-up in Court, your ability to be 'Exact' is paramount to your Defense. When a police officer documents a call or incident, they write in-depth narratives pertaining to all the facts. They make sure to mention ANYTHING they may need to remember in Court even if that something is minor. They do this because of the likelihood that they won't be called-on to testify to those facts for many years and that's the same reason you should. Its important to understand that you will NOT remember important past thoughts and concepts, years down the road, especially while experiencing the stresses of a Criminal or Civil legal proceeding.

So make sure you develop the habit of note taking now. It takes but a few minutes today to protect against a devastating lose tomorrow. You might prefer to make a digital copy of your note via PDF or scanner. Either way you'll want to indicate this in the 'Summery Section' of the Notes Log, then retain this file in the 'Notes Section' of your *ZuluShield Archive* or *Zdrive*.

Contacts Logs:

The primary function of this section is to provide a detailed list of important contacts who will weigh heavily on your ability to initiate a bulletproof Legal Defense when that time comes. Gathering this information today is critical, as it will save enormous headache tomorrow, when you're trying to throw everything together in the eleventh hour.

Here is a breakdown of the Contacts Logs:

1. **The 'Attorneys Log':** This is where you strategically provide yourself the ability to not only find future attorney's, but also to give your attorney points-of-contact for other attorney's, who have real-world experience defending Self-Defense claims. This is HUGE in that it gives your attorney the ability to strategize and bounce ideas off other professionals so as to design the most solid Legal Defense possible. Don't be foolish to assume your attorney knows the best way to defend you. When you come across a real-world Self-Defense claim, do some research and find the actual attorney associated with that case and document them. Self-Defense claims are the most complicated cases to defend, encouraging your attorney to seek peer-council is a great way to add resiliency to your overall legal strategy. Now don't forget, you're going to need a list of BOTH Criminal and Civil Defense attorneys.

2. **The 'Experts Log':** This is where you strategically provide yourself the ability to give your attorney points-of-contact on actual Experts in the field of Self-Defense or Firearms and Tactics. These are the real-world practitioners like, firearms instructors, Force Science specialists and others who have the ability to not only testify on your Defense, but help guide your attorney in developing realistic arguments to counter your accuser's claims. This is HUGE in that it gives your attorney the ability to strategize and bounce ideas off other professionals, so as to design the most solid Legal Defense possible. When you learn of an expert you believe may be of important to your Legal Defense, retain their information. You should do this for EVERY instructor whose class you attend. Don't be foolish to assume your attorney knows the best way to defend you. Self-Defense claims are the most complicated cases to defend, encouraging

your attorney to seek expert council is a great way to add resiliency to your overall legal strategy.

3. **The 'Classmates Log':** This is where you strategically provide yourself the ability to give your attorney points of contact on actual classmates who attended training events you participated in. Classmates are actually a treasure trove of information and can be used to support your Defense in that they can be called on to be a kind of personal reference to you and give testimony as to their reaction to a similar circumstance. Remember your goal is to convince a Judge and Jury that your actions are reasonable to the average person. What better way to do this than with a like-minded individual who attended the same training as you? This is HUGE in that it gives your attorney the ability to embolden your Defense through the testimony of like-minded individuals. Don't be foolish to assume your attorney knows the best way to defend you. Self-Defense claims are the most complicated cases to defend, encouraging your attorney to use secondary references sources is a great way to add resiliency to your overall legal strategy.

4. **The 'References Log':** This is where you strategically provide yourself the ability to give your attorney points-of-contact of Personal References wo can be used to testify in your Defense. Your goal is to convince the Jude and Jury that you are a reasonably mined person; of good character, who's mature and an all-around good person. You'll <u>NEED</u> people who have known you over the course of your life, to testify to their individual perspectives of who you are and what makes you you. Your attorney will ask for a list just like this, so why not start it now instead of racking your brain later, while you're under enormous stress?

Practical Exercise 1:

1. For starters, complete a detailed Incident Report of the June 21st 2013 Millburn New Jersey 'Nanny Cam Home Invasion'. A video of the incident can be found on YouTube (*https://youtu.be/qUOEJS3cJIc*). You will also find numerous news reports of the incident itself, the eventual arrest of the suspect and his sentencing and a ton of background. Be sure to document the facts of the incident, your feelings about it and any important information you believe should be gleaned from this incident. Remember you're writing from a Preemptive Perspective, where your intent is to use this particular incident as supportive evidence in the likelihood that you'll one day be faced with your own real-world Home Invasion attempt at your home and will you choose to defend yourself as apposed to be viciously attacked like this poor lady. Be as detailed as possible. Make sure to reference each fact or thought, with the particular sources of that information, such as individual news articles, commentaries or how they may relate to other similar incidents. Then make sure to capture the actual reports, articles and or commentaries you've referenced and retain them. You might prefer to make a digital copy of this information and your report via PDF or scanner. Either way you'll want to indicate this in the 'Summery Section' of the Literary or Notes Log, then retain this file in its respective section of your *ZuluShield Archive* or *Zdrive*. You'll also need to create an entry on a Multi-Media Log and download the Nanny Cam video to the Multi-Media Section of your *Zdrive*.

2. Complete a detailed Incident Report of the July 23rd 2007 Cheshire, Connecticut Home Invasion incident. This incident is so infamous that it has its own dedicated Wikipedia page. You will also find numerous news reports of the incident itself, the eventual arrest of the suspects and their sentencing and a ton of background information. Be sure to document the facts of the incident, your feelings about it and any important information you believe should be gleaned from this incident. Remember you're writing from a Preemptive Perspective, where your intent is to use this particular incident as supportive evidence in the likelihood that you'll one day be faced with your own real-world Home Invasion attempt at your home and will you choose to defend yourself as apposed to be viciously attacked like this poor family. Be as detailed as possible. Make sure to reference each fact or thought, with the particular sources of that information, such as individual news articles, commentaries or how they may relate to other similar incidents. Then make sure to capture the actual reports, articles and or commentaries you've referenced and retain them. You might prefer to make a digital copy of this information and your report via PDF or scanner. Either way you'll want to indicate this in the 'Summery Section' of the Literary or Notes Log, then retain this file in its respective section of your *ZuluShield Archive* or *Zdrive*. You'll also need to create an entry on a Multi-Media Log for any multi-media data you intend to retain and download them to the Multi-Media Section of your *Zdrive*.

Your next step towards success...

By taking the time to learn about *ZuluShield* and how its revolutionized one's ability to develop a bulletproof Firearms Legal Defense, you've acquired the knowledge you need today to approach tomorrow's Deadly Encounter, with wisdom and preparation. By now you've not only learned how this system works, but you've also taken your first two proactive steps forward by completing the previous Practical Exercise.

Now it's time to develop the 'Habit' of proactive thought. The best way to develop this habit is through 'Activity'. I'm going to leave you with (4) protracted assignments, which you're encouraged to infuse into your daily life. In a very short time, this activity, will undoubtedly form a Launchpad for your Legal Defense. It will install the habit of Proactive Thought, and will develop the lifestyle you'll need to guide your steps to your very own customized bulletproof Firearms Legal Defense.

Practical Exercise 2:

1. Purchase a copy of our *ZuluFight Fight To Win* - Home-based firearms training system. The vast majority of firearms training inadvertently sets its trainees up for mortal failure, when it comes to the realities of a real-life Deadly Encounter. *ZuluFight* is truly the Kata of Firearms Self-Defense. It provides the most practical and inexpensive means of training, which can be achieved from the comforts of your own home with no trips to the firearms range. With *ZuluFight* you'll not only learn why 'Dry-Fire' training is guaranteed to develop the most practical and realistic response to a Deadly Threat, but you'll also see why *ZuluFight* takes Dry-Fire Training to a whole other world of firearms

mastery. Simply turn to our handy *ZuluFight* QR Code on Page (284) or visit *www.zulutactical.com/zulufight* to find your *ZuluFight* copy today.

2. Purchase a copy of Lt. Col Dave Grossman's best seller 'On Killing'. When it comes to studying this book, it's important to approach it from the perspective of a 'Student' of the craft. In the same way an MIT Scholar would study a particular source of research material, tare into it and soak it in so as to develop a 'Thesis'. Use this as an opportunity to 'Learn' and glean from the wisdom of the leading expert of Deadly Encounters. As you read it, treat it as an assignment, take notes and think 'Through' the concepts and theories presented. Then compose a book report. Remember you're writing from a Preemptive Perspective, where your intent is to use this particular source of information as supportive evidence in the likelihood that you'll one day be forced to defend yourself. Be as detailed as possible. Make sure to reference each fact or thought, with the particular sources of that information and or chapter you've drawn it from. You might prefer to make a digital copy of your report via PDF or scanner. Either way you'll want to indicate this in the 'Summery Section' of a Literary Log, then retain this data in its respective section in your *ZuluShield Archive* or *Zdrive*. The jewels of wisdom you'll acquire from this book will greatly impact both tomorrow's Tactical and Legal response to a Deadly Threat. Go to *Killology.com/books* and secure your copy of 'On Killing' today!

3. Purchase a copy of Lt. Col Dave Grossman's best seller 'On Combat'. When it comes to studying this book, it's important to approach it from the perspective of a 'Student' of the craft. In the same way an MIT Scholar would study a particular source of research material, tare into it and soak it in so as to develop a 'Thesis'. Use this as an opportunity to 'Learn' and glean from the wisdom of the leading expert of Deadly Encounters. As you read it, treat it as an assignment, take notes and think 'Through' the concepts and theories presented. Then compose a book report. Remember you're writing from a Preemptive Perspective, where your intent is to use this particular source of information as supportive evidence in the likelihood that you'll one day be forced to defend yourself. Be as detailed as possible. Make sure to reference each fact or thought, with the particular sources of that information and or chapter you've drawn it from. You might prefer to make a digital copy of your report via PDF or scanner. Either way you'll want to indicate this in the 'Summery Section' of a Literary Log, then retain this data in its respective section in your *ZuluShield Archive* or *Zdrive*. The jewels of wisdom you'll acquire from this book will greatly impact both tomorrow's Tactical and Legal response to a Deadly Threat. Go to *Killology.com/books* and secure your copy of 'On Combat' today!

4. Purchase a copy of Lt. Col Dave Grossman's best seller 'Warrior Mindset'. When it comes to studying this book, it's important to approach it from the perspective of a 'Student' of the craft. In the same way an MIT Scholar would study a particular source of research material, tare into it and soak it in so as to develop a 'Thesis'. Use this as an opportunity to 'Learn' and glean from the wisdom of the leading expert of Deadly Encounters. As you read it, treat it as an assignment, take notes and think 'Through' the concepts and theories presented. Then compose a book report. Remember you're writing from a

Preemptive Perspective, where your intent is to use this particular source of information as supportive evidence in the likelihood that you'll one day be forced to defend yourself. Be as detailed as possible. Make sure to reference each fact or thought, with the particular sources of that information and or chapter you've drawn it from. You might prefer to make a digital copy of your report via PDF or scanner. Either way you'll want to indicate this in the 'Summery Section' of a Literary Log, then retain this data in its respective section in your *ZuluShield Archive* or *Zdrive*. The jewels of wisdom you'll acquire from this book will greatly impact both tomorrow's Tactical and Legal response to a Deadly Threat. Go to *Killology.com/books* and secure your copy of 'Warrior Mindset' today!

The objective behind these assignments, is to properly secure tomorrow's Legal Defense on solid bedrock. It's critical that you approach each assignment as an opportunity to 'Learn' and 'Report'. *ZuluFight* gives you the ability to gain the most scientifically proven method of developing instantaneous kinesthetic responses to Deadly Threats. It also gives you the ability to report on the progression of your training, as will as provide a breadcrumb trail of said training, which will be huge when it comes time to defend your actions tomorrow.

The book studies are just as vital. These three books are the stand-alone pillars of the science of Deadly Encounters. Infusing them into your Legal Defense will allow you to reinforce the foundations, much like an architect uses rebar and iron beams to strengthen the foundations of a skyscraper. Take your time and study with the expectation that the knowledge you learn through the process of studying these books, WILL save your bacon tomorrow both Tactically and Legally.

Ready.... Set..... GO!

Now that you have your first two entries under your belt. You've also begun a much more in-depth study into the dynamics and science behind Firearms Self-Defense. Now its time to expand your horizons even further. The intent of *ZuluShield* is to take Proactive Steps towards that day when your use of Self-Defense will be scrutinized. You do this by gathering vital information today, which you will use to defend your future actions. That means you need to put your own self-motivated effort into your future Legal Defense. Nobody else is going to do this for you.

Put it like this, you purchased a firearm for Self-Defense. You train with it and carry it because you believe in your heart of hearts, you will actually need it some day. But when that 'Someday' comes, are you expecting to pull your firearm out and wait for a passerby to pull the trigger for you? No of course not! In order for you to have the very best most bulletproof Firearms Legal Defense tomorrow, you need to begin the process of squeezing that trigger today. You need continue the process of squeezing an preparing for 'Someday'... today. You simply can't afford to wait until tomorrow.

Now if you're like the average person, then your time is pretty limited. However, 'Time' is what you make of it and how you prioritize it. If you're truly concerned about protecting yourself, then you'll make the time to put in time. So that you avoid putting this task off and get lost in last year's unaccomplished resolutions, I suggest dedicating a (1) hour block each week, which you use for *ZuluProofing*. Make sure it's the same hour on the same day of the week and stay consistent. You'll be surprised at just how much you'll accomplish in that short period of time. Use this time to randomly search a particular topic or find one you heard about earlier that week. Then complete a report and or download or print a copy and file it in its respective place in your *ZuluShield Archive or Zdrive*. Before long this will become a habit you'll use for the rest of your days. Remember, much of what you'll be researching are real-world incidents, not only will this help harden up your Legal Defense, but it will also condition your psyche on what to expect in the real-world and in turn your *ZuluProofing* sessions will impact your training to better focus that training on realistic, practical responses, which are both Tactically and Legally sound.

Keep your eyes peeled and your ears tuned as you go about your days. When you hear a report on the radio or see one in the news, take note of this. Then during your next *ZuluProofing* session, find that particular article or incident and document it accordingly. There are two ways I accomplish this throughout a given week:

1. Smartphones are great because of the cool apps available. One app I use a lot of is Evernote. Its an internet based note taking app which offers a very wide range of documentation options to include inserting URLs and videos as well as normal word processing formatting. What's more you can sync your phone app with your Evernote internet cloud so you never lose those important thoughts. This also streamlines the process of sending this information to your main computer when it comes time to *ZuluProof*. All you do is simply log-in to your Evernote account and like magic, all those notes you made throughout a given week, are now on your main computer.

   I set-up my Evernote system so that it mimics *ZuluShield* in that I have folders for 'Notes', 'Multi-Media', 'Literary' and so on. When I come across something on any given day, I either copy and past the URL, YouTube or simply make note of the incident, then file it accordingly in my Evernote system. Then when it's time to *ZuluProof*, I simply log on to my Evernote account from my main computer and wallah, its there.

2. Another way to stay alert is through Facebook. Most of us brows our News Feed multiple times a day. That makes for a great opportunity to find *ZuluShield* worthy information. When you come upon something of value, save it. Say the Facebook post leads to a blog article on a particular Self-Defense topic. Simply copy and paste the URL from that blog or website into an Evernote note, file that note in it's appropriate folder and you've got it right where you need it for your next *ZuluProofing* session. You can increase the frequency of finding *ZuluShield* worth posts by liking Facebook pages of places like Concealed Nation, the NRA, Guns & Ammo, Krav Maga Global and other firearms related blogs.

Here are a few other places you should search:

1. **ZuluShield Facebook Page:** Like our Facebook page at *www.facebook/zulushield* where you'll find ZuluShield worthy information hand-picked by our team. Always remember that these posts are a 'Starting Point'. Should you find interest in a particular incident cited, do your homework and research that incident further. Find-out everything you can about that incident now, so you'll have it tomorrow. You'll also notice that many of our posts are 'Shares' form third-party blogs, companies or groups, find their Facebook page and follow them. If we're sharing their posts on our page, it must mean they know what they're talking about. Doing so will add the variety of 'Perspective' you need to better balance your Firearms Legal Defense.

2. **The NRA:** join the NRA and subscribe to their magazines and link-in with their Facebook pages. They have a huge network of very well informed individuals who post some very well put together commentaries on the subject of Firearms Self-Defense as well as some great reviews on firearms equipment, which will aid you in your quest to develop the most practical response tomorrow.

3. **USA Carry:** has a plethora of information and resources from on-going blogs about real-world incidents, to important statistical data and resources galore on Self-Defense attorney's and insurance, training opportunities and an extremely accurate interactive map, which shows you the firearms laws for each state to include Concealed Carry Reciprocity. Make sure to follow their Facebook. This is one place you DON'T want to overlook.

4. **Concealed Nation:** is an enormous source of information. Linking yourself to their Facebook will assure that you regularly have *ZuluShield* worthy posts streaming across your News Feed daily. In any given day they my highlight two or three real-world incidents involving Firearms Self-Defense as well as training and other important factors to defeating an attack.

5. **First Person Defender:** you'll find these guys on YouTube and they're a resource you simply can't afford to overlook. They specialize in 'Force on Force Simulation Training' which is hands down the BEST way to train your body and mind for Deadly Encounters. You are encouraged to seek out this real-world hands on training yourself as it will greatly increase your ability to defeat a violent attack tomorrow. In the meantime, brows their YouTube videos and spend some time watching them. Each individual video is a learning opportunity on tactics as well as the realities of Deadly Encounters. In Chapter (3) we had an extremely in-depth discussion of the topic of 'Force Science'. First Person Defender turns words on paper into real-world action for an unforgettable visual lesson in what really happens in a real-world confrontation. Again these guys are an amazing source of information. I suggest doing book reports on each video. No you don't have to do it all at once, just periodically. Trust me these are the types of things that you'll NEED when it comes time do defend your use of Self-Defense tomorrow.

6. **Krav Maga Global:** I am a huge supporter of Krav Maga and believe it is hands down the MOST realistic hand-to-hand Self-Defense system around. I'm not saying that other similar martial arts forms like Jujitsu aren't effective in the real-world, I'm simply saying that Krav Maga is better suited for real-life fights, while others are better suited for the 'Sport' of martial arts. There's a reason why our entire Special Operations Community has switched to Krav Maga

infused systems. The founders of Krav Maga determined to develop a system of Self-Defense, which provides the most immediate and deadly response possible, capable of ending the fight in the shortest period of time, so you can survive the day and go home to your family. They gleaned from all other martial art forms and selected only the most 'Practical' moves and techniques which actually work in real-life confrontations. In a real fight, the winner gets to breath another day. A real-life confrontation has nothing to do with take-down points or 'Tap-Outs' its about defending life itself. Go to their homepage, create an account and learn about Krav Maga opportunities in your area. Go to their Facebook page and follow them. Like First Person Defender, you'll find the Krav Maga network to be an amazing source of tons of extremely useful information.

7. **Killology Research Group**: Lt. Col Dave Grossman is hands down the leading expert of armed Deadly Encounters. He dedicated his entire career in the study of conflict from the perspective of a scientist. His intent was to find patterns of probability so as to better define what works and what doesn't work when it relates to developing battle strategies for CQB Combat scenarios. His work took him to a depth of understanding on the subject that we're only now beginning to understand. He's simply light-years ahead of the curve and someone you NEED to pay attention to. There's a reason he was the Director of the US Army Warrior Science Group and why EVERY Special Operations group in the world, tunes in to his station. Go to his home page at *Killoloty.com*, you'll find him to be an enormous source of vital information.

8. **Force Science Institute**: In Chapter (3) we discussed the science of conflict called Force Science and went through an extremely in-depth study of it's foundational concepts. The number one greatest overlooked aspect of Firearms Legal Defense boils down to 'Reality'. Essentially your 'Actions' are what will be judged, so how better to determine if a particular action is reasonable than to weigh said action or shall I say 're-action' with science. Force Science is clear, there are truths as factual as Sir Isaac Newton's 'Laws of Physics' and Einstein's 'Theory of Relativity'. As real as Gravity is to you and that absent some supernatural higher power, you'll NEVER walk on water or sprout wings and fly, there are realities of human conflict which MUST be considered when determining your Defense strategy. Sadly, the vast majority of our nation's top defense attorney's haven't a clue when it comes to how Force Science relates to Self-Defense. So it's up to you to infuse tomorrow's Legal Defense with 'Science' and prove your re-action to tomorrow's deadly attack is not only reasonable but backed by irrefutable science. Take some time and visit their homepage at *Forcescience.org*. Learn about up-coming events and check-out their 'Articles Section', where you'll find a substantial source of the most scientific studies on Deadly Force Encounters.

Prepared for disaster

Out East you get hurricanes. In the Midwest, tornados and in the West we get earthquakes. Preparing for any natural disaster is an extremely sobering task because you soon realize just how out-of-control the future event truly is. You have no way of knowing exactly what to expect except to gauge its probability on past occurrences. However, there is a sense of calm one experiences once they've developed a plan and have acquired adequate provisions to survive such an out-of-control occurrence. This also includes its aftermath. Being prepared gives you both the wisdom; on the best path forward, as well as the ability to mitigate any likely outcome and that gives you the peace-of-mind to approach tomorrow with confidence.

Now what?

By now you've realized that it's not 'If' but <u>WHEN</u> you'll be faced with the life or death decision on whether you should defend your life and exactly how you're going to initiate that Defense. To shoot or not to shoot, a question on the minds of all armed-professionals and armed-citizens alike. While others approach this likelihood from a naïve perspective of being unprepared, with *ZuluShield*, you've been given the opportunity of a perspective based on wisdom and preparation. With *ZuluShield* you now have the ability of knowing how to infuse 'Reason' into tomorrow's instinctive response to a Deadly Threat, by using strategy of 'Thought' today. With *ZuluShield* you have the means to proceed with confidence because you know that <u>WHEN</u> that day comes and you're forced to use Self-Defense, you've prepared for the battle and the legal war that follows. Because it's not 'If' but <u>WHEN</u> and with *ZuluShield* you're ready!

The most important thing is that you stick with it. Don't get lazy and don't forget to *Reload* when you need to. Commit yourself today to the *ZuluShield* process. Trust me, should you become the focus of a Homicide investigation or find yourself on the receiving end of a Wrongful Death lawsuit, all for legitimately defending yourself from a violent attack, you'll be thanking your lucky stars you stayed *Zulu*. Simply turn to our handy *ZuluShield* QR Code on Page (284) or visit *www.zulutactical.com/zulushield* to find all our *ZuluShield* products. Whatever you do, get protected and stay *Zulu*.

The particular degree of resiliency your Firearms Legal Defense has tomorrow, completely depends on the amount of focus you place on it today. It boils down to 'Prioritization', how one thing has precedence over the other. If you don't make your Legal Defense a priority, it won't be. However, if you develop the habit of being ready 'Today', you will be.

Allow me to be your crystal ball.... You <u>WILL</u> end up being forced to defend yourself at some point in your life. That use of Self-Defense, <u>WILL</u> be scrutinized and you <u>WILL</u> be the focus of a Criminal Investigation. There <u>WILL</u> also be Civil ramifications of that incident and you <u>WILL</u> need the information you'll have acquired, documented and retained in this system. It's not an 'If' but WHEN. Now that you know the future, do something about it.

LICENSES

Concealed Carry List

Place an (x) beside States or Territories you're licensed to Concealed Carry in

	Alabama
	Alaska
	Arizona
	Arkansas
	California
	Colorado
	Connecticut
	Delaware
	District of Columbia
	Florida
	Georgia
	Hawaii
	Idaho
	Illinois
	Indiana
	Iowa
	Kansas
	Kentucky
	Louisiana
	Maine
	Maryland
	Massachusetts
	Michigan
	Minnesota
	Mississippi
	Missouri
	Montana
	Nebraska

	Nevada
	New Hampshire
	New Jersey
	New Mexico
	New York
	North Carolina
	North Dakota
	Ohio
	Oklahoma
	Oregon
	Pennsylvania
	Rode Island
	South Carolina
	South Dakota
	Tennessee
	Texas
	Utah
	Vermont
	Virginia
	Washington
	West Virginia
	Wisconsin
	Wyoming
	America Samoa
	Guam
	Northern Marianas Islands
	Puerto Rico

Open Carry List

Place an (x) beside States or Territories you're authorized to Open Carry in

	Alabama
	Alaska
	Arizona
	Arkansas
	California
	Colorado
	Connecticut
	Delaware
	District of Columbia
	Florida
	Georgia
	Hawaii
	Idaho
	Illinois
	Indiana
	Iowa
	Kansas
	Kentucky
	Louisiana
	Maine
	Maryland
	Massachusetts
	Michigan
	Minnesota
	Mississippi
	Missouri
	Montana
	Nebraska

	Nevada
	New Hampshire
	New Jersey
	New Mexico
	New York
	North Carolina
	North Dakota
	Ohio
	Oklahoma
	Oregon
	Pennsylvania
	Rode Island
	South Carolina
	South Dakota
	Tennessee
	Texas
	Utah
	Vermont
	Virginia
	Washington
	West Virginia
	Wisconsin
	Wyoming
	America Samoa
	Guam
	Northern Marianas Islands
	Puerto Rico

Assault Weapons List

Place an (x) beside States or Territories you're authorized to have Assault Weapons in

	Alabama
	Alaska
	Arizona
	Arkansas
	California
	Colorado
	Connecticut
	Delaware
	District of Columbia
	Florida
	Georgia
	Hawaii
	Idaho
	Illinois
	Indiana
	Iowa
	Kansas
	Kentucky
	Louisiana
	Maine
	Maryland
	Massachusetts
	Michigan
	Minnesota
	Mississippi
	Missouri
	Montana
	Nebraska

	Nevada
	New Hampshire
	New Jersey
	New Mexico
	New York
	North Carolina
	North Dakota
	Ohio
	Oklahoma
	Oregon
	Pennsylvania
	Rode Island
	South Carolina
	South Dakota
	Tennessee
	Texas
	Utah
	Vermont
	Virginia
	Washington
	West Virginia
	Wisconsin
	Wyoming
	America Samoa
	Guam
	Northern Marianas Islands
	Puerto Rico

Unrestricted Magazines List

Place an (x) beside States or Territories where there's NO restrictions on magazine capacity

	Alabama			Nevada
	Alaska			New Hampshire
	Arizona			New Jersey
	Arkansas			New Mexico
	California			New York
	Colorado			North Carolina
	Connecticut			North Dakota
	Delaware			Ohio
	District of Columbia			Oklahoma
	Florida			Oregon
	Georgia			Pennsylvania
	Hawaii			Rode Island
	Idaho			South Carolina
	Illinois			South Dakota
	Indiana			Tennessee
	Iowa			Texas
	Kansas			Utah
	Kentucky			Vermont
	Louisiana			Virginia
	Maine			Washington
	Maryland			West Virginia
	Massachusetts			Wisconsin
	Michigan			Wyoming
	Minnesota			America Samoa
	Mississippi			Guam
	Missouri			Northern Marianas Islands
	Montana			Puerto Rico
	Nebraska			

Licenses Log

Title	
Issue Date	/ /

	Expiration Date	/ /

Title	
Issue Date	/ /

	Expiration Date	/ /

Title	
Issue Date	/ /

	Expiration Date	/ /

Title	
Issue Date	/ /

	Expiration Date	/ /

Title	
Issue Date	/ /

	Expiration Date	/ /

Title	
Issue Date	/ /

	Expiration Date	/ /

Title	
Issue Date	/ /

	Expiration Date	/ /

Title	
Issue Date	/ /

	Expiration Date	/ /

Title	
Issue Date	/ /

	Expiration Date	/ /

Title	
Issue Date	/ /

	Expiration Date	/ /

Title	
Issue Date	/ /

	Expiration Date	/ /

Title	
Issue Date	/ /

	Expiration Date	/ /

Licenses Log

Title	
Issue Date	/ /	Expiration Date	/ /

Title	
Issue Date	/ /	Expiration Date	/ /

Title	
Issue Date	/ /	Expiration Date	/ /

Title	
Issue Date	/ /	Expiration Date	/ /

Title	
Issue Date	/ /	Expiration Date	/ /

Title	
Issue Date	/ /	Expiration Date	/ /

Title	
Issue Date	/ /	Expiration Date	/ /

Title	
Issue Date	/ /	Expiration Date	/ /

Title	
Issue Date	/ /	Expiration Date	/ /

Title	
Issue Date	/ /	Expiration Date	/ /

Title	
Issue Date	/ /	Expiration Date	/ /

Title	
Issue Date	/ /	Expiration Date	/ /

CERTIFICATES

Certificates Log

Title	
Instructor	
Issuing Entity	Issue Date / /

Title	
Instructor	
Issuing Entity	Issue Date / /

Title	
Instructor	
Issuing Entity	Issue Date / /

Title	
Instructor	
Issuing Entity	Issue Date / /

Title	
Instructor	
Issuing Entity	Issue Date / /

Title	
Instructor	
Issuing Entity	Issue Date / /

Title	
Instructor	
Issuing Entity	Issue Date / /

Title	
Instructor	
Issuing Entity	Issue Date / /

Title	
Instructor	
Issuing Entity	Issue Date / /

Certificates Log

Title			
Instructor			
Issuing Entity		Issue Date	/ /

Title			
Instructor			
Issuing Entity		Issue Date	/ /

Title			
Instructor			
Issuing Entity		Issue Date	/ /

Title			
Instructor			
Issuing Entity		Issue Date	/ /

Title			
Instructor			
Issuing Entity		Issue Date	/ /

Title			
Instructor			
Issuing Entity		Issue Date	/ /

Title			
Instructor			
Issuing Entity		Issue Date	/ /

Title			
Instructor			
Issuing Entity		Issue Date	/ /

Title			
Instructor			
Issuing Entity		Issue Date	/ /

Certificates Log

Title	
Instructor	

Issuing Entity		Issue Date	/ /

Title	
Instructor	

Issuing Entity		Issue Date	/ /

Title	
Instructor	

Issuing Entity		Issue Date	/ /

Title	
Instructor	

Issuing Entity		Issue Date	/ /

Title	
Instructor	

Issuing Entity		Issue Date	/ /

Title	
Instructor	

Issuing Entity		Issue Date	/ /

Title	
Instructor	

Issuing Entity		Issue Date	/ /

Title	
Instructor	

Issuing Entity		Issue Date	/ /

Title	
Instructor	

Issuing Entity		Issue Date	/ /

Certificates Log

Title	
Instructor	
Issuing Entity	Issue Date / /

Title	
Instructor	
Issuing Entity	Issue Date / /

Title	
Instructor	
Issuing Entity	Issue Date / /

Title	
Instructor	
Issuing Entity	Issue Date / /

Title	
Instructor	
Issuing Entity	Issue Date / /

Title	
Instructor	
Issuing Entity	Issue Date / /

Title	
Instructor	
Issuing Entity	Issue Date / /

Title	
Instructor	
Issuing Entity	Issue Date / /

Title	
Instructor	
Issuing Entity	Issue Date / /

TRAINING

Training Log

Date	/ /	Time	:	Type	
Company					
Instructor					
Contact Info					
Certificate	Yes No	Course Fee		Duration	

Notes:

Date	/ /	Time	:	Type	
Company					
Instructor					
Contact Info					
Certificate	Yes No	Course Fee		Duration	

Notes:

Training Log

Date	/ /	Time	:	Type	
Company					
Instructor					
Contact Info					
Certificate	Yes No	Course Fee		Duration	

Notes:

Date	/ /	Time	:	Type	
Company					
Instructor					
Contact Info					
Certificate	Yes No	Course Fee		Duration	

Notes:

Training Log

Date	/ /	Time	:	Type	
Company					
Instructor					
Contact Info					
Certificate	Yes No	Course Fee		Duration	

Notes:

Date	/ /	Time	:	Type	
Company					
Instructor					
Contact Info					
Certificate	Yes No	Course Fee		Duration	

Notes:

Training Log

Date	/ /	Time	:	Type	
Company					
Instructor					
Contact Info					
Certificate	Yes No	Course Fee		Duration	

Notes:

Date	/ /	Time	:	Type	
Company					
Instructor					
Contact Info					
Certificate	Yes No	Course Fee		Duration	

Notes:

Training Log

Date	/ /	Time	:	Type	
Company					
Instructor					
Contact Info					
Certificate	Yes No	Course Fee		Duration	

Notes:

Date	/ /	Time	:	Type	
Company					
Instructor					
Contact Info					
Certificate	Yes No	Course Fee		Duration	

Notes:

Training Log

Date	/ /	Time	:	Type	
Company					
Instructor					
Contact Info					
Certificate	Yes No	Course Fee		Duration	

Notes:

Date	/ /	Time	:	Type	
Company					
Instructor					
Contact Info					
Certificate	Yes No	Course Fee		Duration	

Notes:

Training Log

Date	/ /	Time	:	Type	
Company					
Instructor					
Contact Info					
Certificate	Yes No	Course Fee		Duration	

Notes:

Date	/ /	Time	:	Type	
Company					
Instructor					
Contact Info					
Certificate	Yes No	Course Fee		Duration	

Notes:

Training Log

Date	/ /	Time	:	Type	
Company					
Instructor					
Contact Info					
Certificate	Yes No	Course Fee		Duration	

Notes:

Date	/ /	Time	:	Type	
Company					
Instructor					
Contact Info					
Certificate	Yes No	Course Fee		Duration	

Notes:

Training Log

Date	/ /	Time	:	Type	
Company					
Instructor					
Contact Info					
Certificate	Yes No	Course Fee		Duration	

Notes:

Date	/ /	Time	:	Type	
Company					
Instructor					
Contact Info					
Certificate	Yes No	Course Fee		Duration	

Notes:

Training Log

Date	/ /	Time	:	Type	
Company					
Instructor					
Contact Info					
Certificate	Yes No	Course Fee		Duration	

Notes:

Date	/ /	Time	:	Type	
Company					
Instructor					
Contact Info					
Certificate	Yes No	Course Fee		Duration	

Notes:

Training Log

Date	/ /	Time	:	Type	
Company					
Instructor					
Contact Info					
Certificate	Yes No	Course Fee		Duration	

Notes:

Date	/ /	Time	:	Type	
Company					
Instructor					
Contact Info					
Certificate	Yes No	Course Fee		Duration	

Notes:

Training Log

Date	/ /	Time	:	Type	
Company					
Instructor					
Contact Info					
Certificate	Yes No	Course Fee		Duration	

Notes:

Date	/ /	Time	:	Type	
Company					
Instructor					
Contact Info					
Certificate	Yes No	Course Fee		Duration	

Notes:

Training Log

Date	/ /	Time	:	Type	
Company					
Instructor					
Contact Info					
Certificate	Yes No	Course Fee		Duration	

Notes:

Date	/ /	Time	:	Type	
Company					
Instructor					
Contact Info					
Certificate	Yes No	Course Fee		Duration	

Notes:

Training Log

Date	/ /	Time	:	Type	
Company					
Instructor					
Contact Info					
Certificate	Yes No	Course Fee		Duration	

Notes:

Date	/ /	Time	:	Type	
Company					
Instructor					
Contact Info					
Certificate	Yes No	Course Fee		Duration	

Notes:

Training Log

Date	/ /	Time	:	Type	
Company					
Instructor					
Contact Info					
Certificate	Yes No	Course Fee		Duration	

Notes:

Date	/ /	Time	:	Type	
Company					
Instructor					
Contact Info					
Certificate	Yes No	Course Fee		Duration	

Notes:

Training Log

Date	/ /	Time	:	Type	
Company					
Instructor					
Contact Info					
Certificate	Yes No	Course Fee		Duration	

Notes:

Date	/ /	Time	:	Type	
Company					
Instructor					
Contact Info					
Certificate	Yes No	Course Fee		Duration	

Notes:

Training Log

Date	/ /	Time	:	Type	
Company					
Instructor					
Contact Info					
Certificate	Yes No	Course Fee		Duration	

Notes:

Date	/ /	Time	:	Type	
Company					
Instructor					
Contact Info					
Certificate	Yes No	Course Fee		Duration	

Notes:

Training Log

Date	/ /	Time	:	Type	
Company					
Instructor					
Contact Info					
Certificate	Yes No	Course Fee		Duration	

Notes:

Date	/ /	Time	:	Type	
Company					
Instructor					
Contact Info					
Certificate	Yes No	Course Fee		Duration	

Notes:

Training Log

Date	/ /	Time	:	Type	
Company					
Instructor					
Contact Info					
Certificate	Yes No	Course Fee		Duration	

Notes:

Date	/ /	Time	:	Type	
Company					
Instructor					
Contact Info					
Certificate	Yes No	Course Fee		Duration	

Notes:

Training Log

Date	/ /	Time	:	Type	
Company					
Instructor					
Contact Info					
Certificate	Yes No	Course Fee		Duration	

Notes:

Date	/ /	Time	:	Type	
Company					
Instructor					
Contact Info					
Certificate	Yes No	Course Fee		Duration	

Notes:

Training Log

Date	/ /	Time	:	Type	
Company					
Instructor					
Contact Info					
Certificate	Yes No	Course Fee		Duration	

Notes:

Date	/ /	Time	:	Type	
Company					
Instructor					
Contact Info					
Certificate	Yes No	Course Fee		Duration	

Notes:

Training Log

Date	/ /	Time	:	Type	
Company					
Instructor					
Contact Info					
Certificate	Yes No	Course Fee		Duration	

Notes:

Date	/ /	Time	:	Type	
Company					
Instructor					
Contact Info					
Certificate	Yes No	Course Fee		Duration	

Notes:

Training Log

Date	/ /	Time	:	Type	
Company					
Instructor					
Contact Info					
Certificate	Yes No	Course Fee		Duration	

Notes:

Date	/ /	Time	:	Type	
Company					
Instructor					
Contact Info					
Certificate	Yes No	Course Fee		Duration	

Notes:

Training Log

Date	/ /	Time	:	Type	
Company					
Instructor					
Contact Info					
Certificate	Yes No	Course Fee		Duration	

Notes:

Date	/ /	Time	:	Type	
Company					
Instructor					
Contact Info					
Certificate	Yes No	Course Fee		Duration	

Notes:

Training Log

Date	/ /	Time	:	Type	
Company					
Instructor					
Contact Info					
Certificate	Yes No	Course Fee		Duration	

Notes:

Date	/ /	Time	:	Type	
Company					
Instructor					
Contact Info					
Certificate	Yes No	Course Fee		Duration	

Notes:

Training Log

Date	/ /	Time	:	Type	
Company					
Instructor					
Contact Info					
Certificate	Yes No	Course Fee		Duration	

Notes:

Date	/ /	Time	:	Type	
Company					
Instructor					
Contact Info					
Certificate	Yes No	Course Fee		Duration	

Notes:

Training Log

Date	/ /	Time	:	Type	
Company					
Instructor					
Contact Info					
Certificate	Yes No	Course Fee		Duration	

Notes:

Date	/ /	Time	:	Type	
Company					
Instructor					
Contact Info					
Certificate	Yes No	Course Fee		Duration	

Notes:

Training Log

Date	/ /	Time	:	Type	
Company					
Instructor					
Contact Info					
Certificate	Yes No	Course Fee		Duration	

Notes:

Date	/ /	Time	:	Type	
Company					
Instructor					
Contact Info					
Certificate	Yes No	Course Fee		Duration	

Notes:

Training Log

Date	/ /	Time	:	Type	
Company					
Instructor					
Contact Info					
Certificate	Yes No	Course Fee		Duration	

Notes:

Date	/ /	Time	:	Type	
Company					
Instructor					
Contact Info					
Certificate	Yes No	Course Fee		Duration	

Notes:

Training Log

Date	/ /	Time	:	Type	
Company					
Instructor					
Contact Info					
Certificate	Yes No	Course Fee		Duration	

Notes:

Date	/ /	Time	:	Type	
Company					
Instructor					
Contact Info					
Certificate	Yes No	Course Fee		Duration	

Notes:

Training Log

Date	/ /	Time	:	Type	
Company					
Instructor					
Contact Info					
Certificate	Yes No	Course Fee		Duration	

Notes:

Date	/ /	Time	:	Type	
Company					
Instructor					
Contact Info					
Certificate	Yes No	Course Fee		Duration	

Notes:

Training Log

Date	/ /	Time	:	Type	
Company					
Instructor					
Contact Info					
Certificate	Yes No	Course Fee		Duration	

Notes:

Date	/ /	Time	:	Type	
Company					
Instructor					
Contact Info					
Certificate	Yes No	Course Fee		Duration	

Notes:

Training Log

Date	/ /	Time	:	Type	
Company					
Instructor					
Contact Info					
Certificate	Yes No	Course Fee		Duration	

Notes:

Date	/ /	Time	:	Type	
Company					
Instructor					
Contact Info					
Certificate	Yes No	Course Fee		Duration	

Notes:

Training Log

Date	/ /	Time	:	Type	
Company					
Instructor					
Contact Info					
Certificate	Yes No	Course Fee		Duration	

Notes:

Date	/ /	Time	:	Type	
Company					
Instructor					
Contact Info					
Certificate	Yes No	Course Fee		Duration	

Notes:

Training Log

Date	/ /	Time	:	Type	
Company					
Instructor					
Contact Info					
Certificate	Yes No	Course Fee		Duration	

Notes:

Date	/ /	Time	:	Type	
Company					
Instructor					
Contact Info					
Certificate	Yes No	Course Fee		Duration	

Notes:

Training Log

Date	/ /	Time	:	Type	
Company					
Instructor					
Contact Info					
Certificate	Yes No	Course Fee		Duration	

Notes:

Date	/ /	Time	:	Type	
Company					
Instructor					
Contact Info					
Certificate	Yes No	Course Fee		Duration	

Notes:

Training Log

Date	/ /	Time	:	Type	
Company					
Instructor					
Contact Info					
Certificate	Yes No	Course Fee		Duration	

Notes:

Date	/ /	Time	:	Type	
Company					
Instructor					
Contact Info					
Certificate	Yes No	Course Fee		Duration	

Notes:

Training Log

Date	/ /	Time	:	Type	
Company					
Instructor					
Contact Info					
Certificate	Yes No	Course Fee		Duration	

Notes:

Date	/ /	Time	:	Type	
Company					
Instructor					
Contact Info					
Certificate	Yes No	Course Fee		Duration	

Notes:

Training Log

Date	/ /	Time	:	Type	
Company					
Instructor					
Contact Info					
Certificate	Yes No	Course Fee		Duration	

Notes:

Date	/ /	Time	:	Type	
Company					
Instructor					
Contact Info					
Certificate	Yes No	Course Fee		Duration	

Notes:

Training Log

Date	/ /	Time	:	Type	
Company					
Instructor					
Contact Info					
Certificate	Yes No	Course Fee		Duration	

Notes:

Date	/ /	Time	:	Type	
Company					
Instructor					
Contact Info					
Certificate	Yes No	Course Fee		Duration	

Notes:

Training Log

Date	/ /	Time	:	Type	
Company					
Instructor					
Contact Info					
Certificate	Yes No	Course Fee		Duration	

Notes:

Date	/ /	Time	:	Type	
Company					
Instructor					
Contact Info					
Certificate	Yes No	Course Fee		Duration	

Notes:

Training Log

Date	/ /	Time	:	Type	
Company					
Instructor					
Contact Info					
Certificate	Yes No	Course Fee		Duration	

Notes:

Date	/ /	Time	:	Type	
Company					
Instructor					
Contact Info					
Certificate	Yes No	Course Fee		Duration	

Notes:

Training Log

Date	/ /	Time	:	Type	
Company					
Instructor					
Contact Info					
Certificate	Yes No	Course Fee		Duration	

Notes:

Date	/ /	Time	:	Type	
Company					
Instructor					
Contact Info					
Certificate	Yes No	Course Fee		Duration	

Notes:

Training Log

Date	/ /	Time	:	Type	
Company					
Instructor					
Contact Info					
Certificate	Yes No	Course Fee		Duration	

Notes:

Date	/ /	Time	:	Type	
Company					
Instructor					
Contact Info					
Certificate	Yes No	Course Fee		Duration	

Notes:

Training Log

Date	/ /	Time	:	Type	
Company					
Instructor					
Contact Info					
Certificate	Yes No	Course Fee		Duration	

Notes:

Date	/ /	Time	:	Type	
Company					
Instructor					
Contact Info					
Certificate	Yes No	Course Fee		Duration	

Notes:

Training Log

Date	/ /	Time	:	Type	
Company					
Instructor					
Contact Info					
Certificate	Yes No	Course Fee		Duration	

Notes:

Date	/ /	Time	:	Type	
Company					
Instructor					
Contact Info					
Certificate	Yes No	Course Fee		Duration	

Notes:

Training Log

Date	/ /	Time	:	Type	
Company					
Instructor					
Contact Info					
Certificate	Yes No	Course Fee		Duration	

Notes:

Date	/ /	Time	:	Type	
Company					
Instructor					
Contact Info					
Certificate	Yes No	Course Fee		Duration	

Notes:

Training Log

Date	/ /	Time	:	Type	
Company					
Instructor					
Contact Info					
Certificate	Yes No	Course Fee		Duration	

Notes:

Date	/ /	Time	:	Type	
Company					
Instructor					
Contact Info					
Certificate	Yes No	Course Fee		Duration	

Notes:

Training Log

Date	/ /	Time	:	Type	
Company					
Instructor					
Contact Info					
Certificate	Yes No	Course Fee		Duration	

Notes:

Date	/ /	Time	:	Type	
Company					
Instructor					
Contact Info					
Certificate	Yes No	Course Fee		Duration	

Notes:

Training Log

Date	/ /	Time	:	Type	
Company					
Instructor					
Contact Info					
Certificate	Yes No	Course Fee		Duration	

Notes:

Date	/ /	Time	:	Type	
Company					
Instructor					
Contact Info					
Certificate	Yes No	Course Fee		Duration	

Notes:

LITERARY

Literary Log

Topic	
Title	
Author	Date Read: / /
Summary	

Topic	
Title	
Author	Date Read: / /
Summary	

Topic	
Title	
Author	Date Read: / /
Summary	

Topic	
Title	
Author	Date Read: / /
Summary	

Literary Log

Topic	
Title	
Author		Date Read	/ /

Summary

Topic	
Title	
Author		Date Read	/ /

Summary

Topic	
Title	
Author		Date Read	/ /

Summary

Topic	
Title	
Author		Date Read	/ /

Summary

Literary Log

Topic	
Title	
Author	Date Read	/ /

Summary

Topic	
Title	
Author	Date Read	/ /

Summary

Topic	
Title	
Author	Date Read	/ /

Summary

Topic	
Title	
Author	Date Read	/ /

Summary

Literary Log

Topic	
Title	
Author		Date Read	/ /
Summary	

Topic	
Title	
Author		Date Read	/ /
Summary	

Topic	
Title	
Author		Date Read	/ /
Summary	

Topic	
Title	
Author		Date Read	/ /
Summary	

Literary Log

Topic	
Title	
Author	Date Read	/ /

Summary

Topic	
Title	
Author	Date Read	/ /

Summary

Topic	
Title	
Author	Date Read	/ /

Summary

Topic	
Title	
Author	Date Read	/ /

Summary

Literary Log

Topic	
Title	
Author	Date Read / /

Summary

Topic	
Title	
Author	Date Read / /

Summary

Topic	
Title	
Author	Date Read / /

Summary

Topic	
Title	
Author	Date Read / /

Summary

Literary Log

Topic	
Title	

Author		Date Read	/ /

Summary

Topic	
Title	

Author		Date Read	/ /

Summary

Topic	
Title	

Author		Date Read	/ /

Summary

Topic	
Title	

Author		Date Read	/ /

Summary

Literary Log

Topic	
Title	
Author	

Date Read	/ /

Summary

Topic	
Title	
Author	

Date Read	/ /

Summary

Topic	
Title	
Author	

Date Read	/ /

Summary

Topic	
Title	
Author	

Date Read	/ /

Summary

Literary Log

Topic	
Title	
Author	Date Read __/__/__

Summary

Topic	
Title	
Author	Date Read __/__/__

Summary

Topic	
Title	
Author	Date Read __/__/__

Summary

Topic	
Title	
Author	Date Read __/__/__

Summary

Literary Log

Topic	
Title	
Author	Date Read	/ /

Summary

Topic	
Title	
Author	Date Read	/ /

Summary

Topic	
Title	
Author	Date Read	/ /

Summary

Topic	
Title	
Author	Date Read	/ /

Summary

Literary Log

Topic	
Title	
Author		Date Read	/ /

Summary

Topic	
Title	
Author		Date Read	/ /

Summary

Topic	
Title	
Author		Date Read	/ /

Summary

Topic	
Title	
Author		Date Read	/ /

Summary

Literary Log

Topic	
Title	
Author	Date Read / /

Summary

Topic	
Title	
Author	Date Read / /

Summary

Topic	
Title	
Author	Date Read / /

Summary

Topic	
Title	
Author	Date Read / /

Summary

Literary Log

Topic	
Title	
Author	Date Read	/ /

Summary

Topic	
Title	
Author	Date Read	/ /

Summary

Topic	
Title	
Author	Date Read	/ /

Summary

Topic	
Title	
Author	Date Read	/ /

Summary

Literary Log

Topic	
Title	
Author	Date Read / /

Summary

Topic	
Title	
Author	Date Read / /

Summary

Topic	
Title	
Author	Date Read / /

Summary

Topic	
Title	
Author	Date Read / /

Summary

Literary Log

Topic	
Title	
Author		Date Read	/ /

Summary

Topic	
Title	
Author		Date Read	/ /

Summary

Topic	
Title	
Author		Date Read	/ /

Summary

Topic	
Title	
Author		Date Read	/ /

Summary

Literary Log

Topic	
Title	
Author		Date Read	/ /

Summary

Topic	
Title	
Author		Date Read	/ /

Summary

Topic	
Title	
Author		Date Read	/ /

Summary

Topic	
Title	
Author		Date Read	/ /

Summary

Literary Log

Topic	
Title	
Author		Date Read	/ /

Summary

Topic	
Title	
Author		Date Read	/ /

Summary

Topic	
Title	
Author		Date Read	/ /

Summary

Topic	
Title	
Author		Date Read	/ /

Summary

Literary Log

Topic	
Title	
Author	Date Read / /

Summary

Topic	
Title	
Author	Date Read / /

Summary

Topic	
Title	
Author	Date Read / /

Summary

Topic	
Title	
Author	Date Read / /

Summary

Literary Log

Topic	
Title	
Author		Date Read	/ /

Summary

Topic	
Title	
Author		Date Read	/ /

Summary

Topic	
Title	
Author		Date Read	/ /

Summary

Topic	
Title	
Author		Date Read	/ /

Summary

Literary Log

Topic	
Title	
Author		Date Read	/ /

Summary

Topic	
Title	
Author		Date Read	/ /

Summary

Topic	
Title	
Author		Date Read	/ /

Summary

Topic	
Title	
Author		Date Read	/ /

Summary

Literary Log

Topic	
Title	
Author	Date Read ___/___/___

Summary

Topic	
Title	
Author	Date Read ___/___/___

Summary

Topic	
Title	
Author	Date Read ___/___/___

Summary

Topic	
Title	
Author	Date Read ___/___/___

Summary

Literary Log

Topic	
Title	
Author		Date Read	/ /

Summary

Topic	
Title	
Author		Date Read	/ /

Summary

Topic	
Title	
Author		Date Read	/ /

Summary

Topic	
Title	
Author		Date Read	/ /

Summary

Literary Log

Topic	
Title	
Author	

	Date Read	/ /

Summary

Topic	
Title	
Author	

	Date Read	/ /

Summary

Topic	
Title	
Author	

	Date Read	/ /

Summary

Topic	
Title	
Author	

	Date Read	/ /

Summary

Literary Log

Topic	
Title	
Author		Date Read	/ /

Summary

Topic	
Title	
Author		Date Read	/ /

Summary

Topic	
Title	
Author		Date Read	/ /

Summary

Topic	
Title	
Author		Date Read	/ /

Summary

Literary Log

Topic	
Title	
Author	

Date Read	/ /

Summary

Topic	
Title	
Author	

Date Read	/ /

Summary

Topic	
Title	
Author	

Date Read	/ /

Summary

Topic	
Title	
Author	

Date Read	/ /

Summary

Literary Log

Topic	
Title	
Author		Date Read	/ /

Summary

Topic	
Title	
Author		Date Read	/ /

Summary

Topic	
Title	
Author		Date Read	/ /

Summary

Topic	
Title	
Author		Date Read	/ /

Summary

Multi-Media

Multi-Media Log

Topic	
Title	
Source	Date Added / /

Summary

Topic	
Title	
Source	Date Added / /

Summary

Topic	
Title	
Source	Date Added / /

Summary

Topic	
Title	
Source	Date Added / /

Summary

Multi-Media Log

Topic	
Title	
Source	Date Added / /

Summary

Topic	
Title	
Source	Date Added / /

Summary

Topic	
Title	
Source	Date Added / /

Summary

Topic	
Title	
Source	Date Added / /

Summary

Multi-Media Log

Topic	
Title	

Source		Date Added	/ /

Summary

Topic	
Title	

Source		Date Added	/ /

Summary

Topic	
Title	

Source		Date Added	/ /

Summary

Topic	
Title	

Source		Date Added	/ /

Summary

Multi-Media Log

Topic	
Title	
Source	Date Added / /

Summary

Topic	
Title	
Source	Date Added / /

Summary

Topic	
Title	
Source	Date Added / /

Summary

Topic	
Title	
Source	Date Added / /

Summary

Multi-Media Log

Topic	
Title	
Source	Date Added / /

Summary

Topic	
Title	
Source	Date Added / /

Summary

Topic	
Title	
Source	Date Added / /

Summary

Topic	
Title	
Source	Date Added / /

Summary

Multi-Media Log

Topic	
Title	
Source	Date Added	/ /

Summary

Topic	
Title	
Source	Date Added	/ /

Summary

Topic	
Title	
Source	Date Added	/ /

Summary

Topic	
Title	
Source	Date Added	/ /

Summary

Multi-Media Log

Topic	
Title	

Source		Date Added	/ /

Summary

Topic	
Title	

Source		Date Added	/ /

Summary

Topic	
Title	

Source		Date Added	/ /

Summary

Topic	
Title	

Source		Date Added	/ /

Summary

Multi-Media Log

Topic	
Title	
Source	Date Added / /

Summary

Topic	
Title	
Source	Date Added / /

Summary

Topic	
Title	
Source	Date Added / /

Summary

Topic	
Title	
Source	Date Added / /

Summary

Multi-Media Log

Topic	
Title	
Source	Date Added / /

Summary

Topic	
Title	
Source	Date Added / /

Summary

Topic	
Title	
Source	Date Added / /

Summary

Topic	
Title	
Source	Date Added / /

Summary

Multi-Media Log

Topic	
Title	
Source	Date Added

		/ /
Summary		

Topic	
Title	
Source	Date Added

		/ /
Summary		

Topic	
Title	
Source	Date Added

		/ /
Summary		

Topic	
Title	
Source	Date Added

		/ /
Summary		

Multi-Media Log

Topic	
Title	
Source	Date Added: / /

Summary

Topic	
Title	
Source	Date Added: / /

Summary

Topic	
Title	
Source	Date Added: / /

Summary

Topic	
Title	
Source	Date Added: / /

Summary

Multi-Media Log

Topic	
Title	
Source	Date Added / /

Summary

Topic	
Title	
Source	Date Added / /

Summary

Topic	
Title	
Source	Date Added / /

Summary

Topic	
Title	
Source	Date Added / /

Summary

Multi-Media Log

Topic	
Title	
Source	Date Added / /
Summary	

Topic	
Title	
Source	Date Added / /
Summary	

Topic	
Title	
Source	Date Added / /
Summary	

Topic	
Title	
Source	Date Added / /
Summary	

Multi-Media Log

Topic	
Title	
Source	Date Added / /

Summary

Topic	
Title	
Source	Date Added / /

Summary

Topic	
Title	
Source	Date Added / /

Summary

Topic	
Title	
Source	Date Added / /

Summary

Multi-Media Log

Topic	
Title	
Source	Date Added / /

Summary

Topic	
Title	
Source	Date Added / /

Summary

Topic	
Title	
Source	Date Added / /

Summary

Topic	
Title	
Source	Date Added / /

Summary

Multi-Media Log

Topic	
Title	
Source		Date Added	/ /

Summary

Topic	
Title	
Source		Date Added	/ /

Summary

Topic	
Title	
Source		Date Added	/ /

Summary

Topic	
Title	
Source		Date Added	/ /

Summary

Multi-Media Log

Topic	
Title	
Source		Date Added	/ /

Summary

Topic	
Title	
Source		Date Added	/ /

Summary

Topic	
Title	
Source		Date Added	/ /

Summary

Topic	
Title	
Source		Date Added	/ /

Summary

Multi-Media Log

Topic	
Title	

Source		Date Added	/ /

Summary

Topic	
Title	

Source		Date Added	/ /

Summary

Topic	
Title	

Source		Date Added	/ /

Summary

Topic	
Title	

Source		Date Added	/ /

Summary

Multi-Media Log

Topic	
Title	
Source	Date Added / /

Summary

Topic	
Title	
Source	Date Added / /

Summary

Topic	
Title	
Source	Date Added / /

Summary

Topic	
Title	
Source	Date Added / /

Summary

Multi-Media Log

Topic	
Title	
Source	Date Added / /

Summary

Topic	
Title	
Source	Date Added / /

Summary

Topic	
Title	
Source	Date Added / /

Summary

Topic	
Title	
Source	Date Added / /

Summary

Multi-Media Log

Topic	
Title	
Source	Date Added / /

Summary

Topic	
Title	
Source	Date Added / /

Summary

Topic	
Title	
Source	Date Added / /

Summary

Topic	
Title	
Source	Date Added / /

Summary

Multi-Media Log

Topic	
Title	
Source	Date Added / /

Summary

Topic	
Title	
Source	Date Added / /

Summary

Topic	
Title	
Source	Date Added / /

Summary

Topic	
Title	
Source	Date Added / /

Summary

Multi-Media Log

Topic	
Title	
Source	Date Added / /
Summary	

Topic	
Title	
Source	Date Added / /
Summary	

Topic	
Title	
Source	Date Added / /
Summary	

Topic	
Title	
Source	Date Added / /
Summary	

Multi-Media Log

Topic	
Title	
Source	Date Added / /

Summary

Topic	
Title	
Source	Date Added / /

Summary

Topic	
Title	
Source	Date Added / /

Summary

Topic	
Title	
Source	Date Added / /

Summary

Multi-Media Log

Topic	
Title	
Source	Date Added / /

Summary

Topic	
Title	
Source	Date Added / /

Summary

Topic	
Title	
Source	Date Added / /

Summary

Topic	
Title	
Source	Date Added / /

Summary

Multi-Media Log

Topic	
Title	
Source	Date Added / /

Summary

Topic	
Title	
Source	Date Added / /

Summary

Topic	
Title	
Source	Date Added / /

Summary

Topic	
Title	
Source	Date Added / /

Summary

Multi-Media Log

Topic	
Title	
Source		Date Added	/ /

Summary

Topic	
Title	
Source		Date Added	/ /

Summary

Topic	
Title	
Source		Date Added	/ /

Summary

Topic	
Title	
Source		Date Added	/ /

Summary

Multi-Media Log

Topic	
Title	
Source	Date Added / /

Summary

Topic	
Title	
Source	Date Added / /

Summary

Topic	
Title	
Source	Date Added / /

Summary

Topic	
Title	
Source	Date Added / /

Summary

NOTES

Notes Log

Topic		Date Added	/ /
Title			
Source			

Summary			

Topic		Date Added	/ /
Title			
Source			

Summary			

Topic		Date Added	/ /
Title			
Source			

Summary			

Topic		Date Added	/ /
Title			
Source			

Summary			

Notes Log

Topic		Date Added	/ /
Title			
Source			
Summary			

Topic		Date Added	/ /
Title			
Source			
Summary			

Topic		Date Added	/ /
Title			
Source			
Summary			

Topic		Date Added	/ /
Title			
Source			
Summary			

Notes Log

Topic		Date Added	/ /
Title			
Source			
Summary			

Topic		Date Added	/ /
Title			
Source			
Summary			

Topic		Date Added	/ /
Title			
Source			
Summary			

Topic		Date Added	/ /
Title			
Source			
Summary			

Notes Log

Topic		Date Added	/ /
Title			
Source			
Summary			

Topic		Date Added	/ /
Title			
Source			
Summary			

Topic		Date Added	/ /
Title			
Source			
Summary			

Topic		Date Added	/ /
Title			
Source			
Summary			

Notes Log

Topic		Date Added	/ /
Title			
Source			

Summary

Topic		Date Added	/ /
Title			
Source			

Summary

Topic		Date Added	/ /
Title			
Source			

Summary

Topic		Date Added	/ /
Title			
Source			

Summary

Notes Log

Topic		Date Added	/ /
Title			
Source			
Summary			

Topic		Date Added	/ /
Title			
Source			
Summary			

Topic		Date Added	/ /
Title			
Source			
Summary			

Topic		Date Added	/ /
Title			
Source			
Summary			

Notes Log

Topic		Date Added	/ /
Title			
Source			

Summary

Topic		Date Added	/ /
Title			
Source			

Summary

Topic		Date Added	/ /
Title			
Source			

Summary

Topic		Date Added	/ /
Title			
Source			

Summary

Notes Log

Topic		Date Added	/ /
Title			
Source			
Summary			

Topic		Date Added	/ /
Title			
Source			
Summary			

Topic		Date Added	/ /
Title			
Source			
Summary			

Topic		Date Added	/ /
Title			
Source			
Summary			

Notes Log

Topic		Date Added	/ /
Title			
Source			
Summary			

Topic		Date Added	/ /
Title			
Source			
Summary			

Topic		Date Added	/ /
Title			
Source			
Summary			

Topic		Date Added	/ /
Title			
Source			
Summary			

Notes Log

Topic		Date Added	/ /
Title			
Source			

Summary

Topic		Date Added	/ /
Title			
Source			

Summary

Topic		Date Added	/ /
Title			
Source			

Summary

Topic		Date Added	/ /
Title			
Source			

Summary

Notes Log

Topic		Date Added	/ /
Title			
Source			
Summary			

Topic		Date Added	/ /
Title			
Source			
Summary			

Topic		Date Added	/ /
Title			
Source			
Summary			

Topic		Date Added	/ /
Title			
Source			
Summary			

Notes Log

Topic		Date Added	/ /
Title			
Source			
Summary			

Topic		Date Added	/ /
Title			
Source			
Summary			

Topic		Date Added	/ /
Title			
Source			
Summary			

Topic		Date Added	/ /
Title			
Source			
Summary			

Notes Log

Topic		Date Added	/ /
Title			
Source			

Summary			

Topic		Date Added	/ /
Title			
Source			

Summary			

Topic		Date Added	/ /
Title			
Source			

Summary			

Topic		Date Added	/ /
Title			
Source			

Summary			

Notes Log

Topic		Date Added	/ /
Title			
Source			
Summary			

Topic		Date Added	/ /
Title			
Source			
Summary			

Topic		Date Added	/ /
Title			
Source			
Summary			

Topic		Date Added	/ /
Title			
Source			
Summary			

Notes Log

Topic		Date Added	/ /
Title			
Source			
Summary			

Topic		Date Added	/ /
Title			
Source			
Summary			

Topic		Date Added	/ /
Title			
Source			
Summary			

Topic		Date Added	/ /
Title			
Source			
Summary			

Notes Log

Topic		Date Added	/ /
Title			
Source			

Summary

Topic		Date Added	/ /
Title			
Source			

Summary

Topic		Date Added	/ /
Title			
Source			

Summary

Topic		Date Added	/ /
Title			
Source			

Summary

Notes Log

Topic		Date Added	/ /
Title			
Source			
Summary			

Topic		Date Added	/ /
Title			
Source			
Summary			

Topic		Date Added	/ /
Title			
Source			
Summary			

Topic		Date Added	/ /
Title			
Source			
Summary			

Notes Log

Topic		Date Added	/ /
Title			
Source			

Summary

Topic		Date Added	/ /
Title			
Source			

Summary

Topic		Date Added	/ /
Title			
Source			

Summary

Topic		Date Added	/ /
Title			
Source			

Summary

Notes Log

Topic		Date Added	/ /
Title			
Source			

Summary

Topic		Date Added	/ /
Title			
Source			

Summary

Topic		Date Added	/ /
Title			
Source			

Summary

Topic		Date Added	/ /
Title			
Source			

Summary

Notes Log

Topic		Date Added	/ /
Title			
Source			

Summary

Topic		Date Added	/ /
Title			
Source			

Summary

Topic		Date Added	/ /
Title			
Source			

Summary

Topic		Date Added	/ /
Title			
Source			

Summary

Notes Log

Topic		Date Added	/ /
Title			
Source			

Summary

Topic		Date Added	/ /
Title			
Source			

Summary

Topic		Date Added	/ /
Title			
Source			

Summary

Topic		Date Added	/ /
Title			
Source			

Summary

Notes Log

Topic		Date Added	/ /
Title			
Source			
Summary			

Topic		Date Added	/ /
Title			
Source			
Summary			

Topic		Date Added	/ /
Title			
Source			
Summary			

Topic		Date Added	/ /
Title			
Source			
Summary			

Notes Log

Topic		Date Added	/ /
Title			
Source			
Summary			

Topic		Date Added	/ /
Title			
Source			
Summary			

Topic		Date Added	/ /
Title			
Source			
Summary			

Topic		Date Added	/ /
Title			
Source			
Summary			

Notes Log

Topic		Date Added	/ /
Title			
Source			

Summary

Topic		Date Added	/ /
Title			
Source			

Summary

Topic		Date Added	/ /
Title			
Source			

Summary

Topic		Date Added	/ /
Title			
Source			

Summary

Notes Log

Topic		Date Added	/ /
Title			
Source			
Summary			

Topic		Date Added	/ /
Title			
Source			
Summary			

Topic		Date Added	/ /
Title			
Source			
Summary			

Topic		Date Added	/ /
Title			
Source			
Summary			

Notes Log

Topic		Date Added	/ /
Title			
Source			

Summary

Topic		Date Added	/ /
Title			
Source			

Summary

Topic		Date Added	/ /
Title			
Source			

Summary

Topic		Date Added	/ /
Title			
Source			

Summary

CONTACTS

Attorneys Log

Name	
Specialty	
Company	
Address	
Phone	**Email**

Name	
Specialty	
Company	
Address	
Phone	**Email**

Name	
Specialty	
Company	
Address	
Phone	**Email**

Name	
Specialty	
Company	
Address	
Phone	**Email**

Name	
Specialty	
Company	
Address	
Phone	**Email**

Name	
Specialty	
Company	
Address	
Phone	**Email**

Attorneys Log

Name	
Specialty	
Company	
Address	
Phone	Email

Name	
Specialty	
Company	
Address	
Phone	Email

Name	
Specialty	
Company	
Address	
Phone	Email

Name	
Specialty	
Company	
Address	
Phone	Email

Name	
Specialty	
Company	
Address	
Phone	Email

Name	
Specialty	
Company	
Address	
Phone	Email

Attorneys Log

Name	
Specialty	
Company	
Address	
Phone	Email

Name	
Specialty	
Company	
Address	
Phone	Email

Name	
Specialty	
Company	
Address	
Phone	Email

Name	
Specialty	
Company	
Address	
Phone	Email

Name	
Specialty	
Company	
Address	
Phone	Email

Name	
Specialty	
Company	
Address	
Phone	Email

Attorneys Log

Name	
Specialty	
Company	
Address	
Phone	Email

Name	
Specialty	
Company	
Address	
Phone	Email

Name	
Specialty	
Company	
Address	
Phone	Email

Name	
Specialty	
Company	
Address	
Phone	Email

Name	
Specialty	
Company	
Address	
Phone	Email

Name	
Specialty	
Company	
Address	
Phone	Email

Attorneys Log

Name	
Specialty	
Company	
Address	
Phone	Email

Name	
Specialty	
Company	
Address	
Phone	Email

Name	
Specialty	
Company	
Address	
Phone	Email

Name	
Specialty	
Company	
Address	
Phone	Email

Name	
Specialty	
Company	
Address	
Phone	Email

Name	
Specialty	
Company	
Address	
Phone	Email

Attorneys Log

Name	
Specialty	
Company	
Address	
Phone	Email

Name	
Specialty	
Company	
Address	
Phone	Email

Name	
Specialty	
Company	
Address	
Phone	Email

Name	
Specialty	
Company	
Address	
Phone	Email

Name	
Specialty	
Company	
Address	
Phone	Email

Name	
Specialty	
Company	
Address	
Phone	Email

Attorneys Log

Name	
Specialty	
Company	
Address	
Phone	Email

Name	
Specialty	
Company	
Address	
Phone	Email

Name	
Specialty	
Company	
Address	
Phone	Email

Name	
Specialty	
Company	
Address	
Phone	Email

Name	
Specialty	
Company	
Address	
Phone	Email

Name	
Specialty	
Company	
Address	
Phone	Email

Attorneys Log

Name	
Specialty	
Company	
Address	
Phone	Email

Name	
Specialty	
Company	
Address	
Phone	Email

Name	
Specialty	
Company	
Address	
Phone	Email

Name	
Specialty	
Company	
Address	
Phone	Email

Name	
Specialty	
Company	
Address	
Phone	Email

Name	
Specialty	
Company	
Address	
Phone	Email

Attorneys Log

Name	
Specialty	
Company	
Address	
Phone	Email

Name	
Specialty	
Company	
Address	
Phone	Email

Name	
Specialty	
Company	
Address	
Phone	Email

Name	
Specialty	
Company	
Address	
Phone	Email

Name	
Specialty	
Company	
Address	
Phone	Email

Name	
Specialty	
Company	
Address	
Phone	Email

Attorneys Log

Name	
Specialty	
Company	
Address	
Phone	Email

Name	
Specialty	
Company	
Address	
Phone	Email

Name	
Specialty	
Company	
Address	
Phone	Email

Name	
Specialty	
Company	
Address	
Phone	Email

Name	
Specialty	
Company	
Address	
Phone	Email

Name	
Specialty	
Company	
Address	
Phone	Email

Experts Log

Name	Instructor Zulu
Specialty	Advanced Firearms Instructor / Use-of-Force & Tactics Expert
Company	Zulu Tactical LLC
Address	PO BOX 164, Canby OR 97013
Phone	855-762-9858

Email	info@zulutactical.com

Name	
Specialty	
Company	
Address	
Phone	

Email	

Name	
Specialty	
Company	
Address	
Phone	

Email	

Name	
Specialty	
Company	
Address	
Phone	

Email	

Name	
Specialty	
Company	
Address	
Phone	

Email	

Name	
Specialty	
Company	
Address	
Phone	

Email	

Experts Log

Name	
Specialty	
Company	
Address	

Phone		Email	

Name	
Specialty	
Company	
Address	

Phone		Email	

Name	
Specialty	
Company	
Address	

Phone		Email	

Name	
Specialty	
Company	
Address	

Phone		Email	

Name	
Specialty	
Company	
Address	

Phone		Email	

Name	
Specialty	
Company	
Address	

Phone		Email	

Experts Log

Name	
Specialty	
Company	
Address	
Phone	Email

Name	
Specialty	
Company	
Address	
Phone	Email

Name	
Specialty	
Company	
Address	
Phone	Email

Name	
Specialty	
Company	
Address	
Phone	Email

Name	
Specialty	
Company	
Address	
Phone	Email

Name	
Specialty	
Company	
Address	
Phone	Email

Experts Log

Name	
Specialty	
Company	
Address	
Phone		Email	

Name	
Specialty	
Company	
Address	
Phone		Email	

Name	
Specialty	
Company	
Address	
Phone		Email	

Name	
Specialty	
Company	
Address	
Phone		Email	

Name	
Specialty	
Company	
Address	
Phone		Email	

Name	
Specialty	
Company	
Address	
Phone		Email	

Experts Log

Name	
Specialty	
Company	
Address	
Phone	Email

Name	
Specialty	
Company	
Address	
Phone	Email

Name	
Specialty	
Company	
Address	
Phone	Email

Name	
Specialty	
Company	
Address	
Phone	Email

Name	
Specialty	
Company	
Address	
Phone	Email

Name	
Specialty	
Company	
Address	
Phone	Email

Experts Log

Name	
Specialty	
Company	
Address	
Phone	Email

Name	
Specialty	
Company	
Address	
Phone	Email

Name	
Specialty	
Company	
Address	
Phone	Email

Name	
Specialty	
Company	
Address	
Phone	Email

Name	
Specialty	
Company	
Address	
Phone	Email

Name	
Specialty	
Company	
Address	
Phone	Email

Experts Log

Name	
Specialty	
Company	
Address	
Phone	Email

Name	
Specialty	
Company	
Address	
Phone	Email

Name	
Specialty	
Company	
Address	
Phone	Email

Name	
Specialty	
Company	
Address	
Phone	Email

Name	
Specialty	
Company	
Address	
Phone	Email

Name	
Specialty	
Company	
Address	
Phone	Email

Experts Log

Name	
Specialty	
Company	
Address	

Phone		Email	

Name	
Specialty	
Company	
Address	

Phone		Email	

Name	
Specialty	
Company	
Address	

Phone		Email	

Name	
Specialty	
Company	
Address	

Phone		Email	

Name	
Specialty	
Company	
Address	

Phone		Email	

Name	
Specialty	
Company	
Address	

Phone		Email	

Experts Log

Name	
Specialty	
Company	
Address	
Phone		Email	

Name	
Specialty	
Company	
Address	
Phone		Email	

Name	
Specialty	
Company	
Address	
Phone		Email	

Name	
Specialty	
Company	
Address	
Phone		Email	

Name	
Specialty	
Company	
Address	
Phone		Email	

Name	
Specialty	
Company	
Address	
Phone		Email	

Experts Log

Name	
Specialty	
Company	
Address	
Phone	Email

Name	
Specialty	
Company	
Address	
Phone	Email

Name	
Specialty	
Company	
Address	
Phone	Email

Name	
Specialty	
Company	
Address	
Phone	Email

Name	
Specialty	
Company	
Address	
Phone	Email

Name	
Specialty	
Company	
Address	
Phone	Email

Classmates Log

Class Name		Date	/ /
Name			
Address			
Phone		Email	

Class Name		Date	/ /
Name			
Address			
Phone		Email	

Class Name		Date	/ /
Name			
Address			
Phone		Email	

Class Name		Date	/ /
Name			
Address			
Phone		Email	

Class Name		Date	/ /
Name			
Address			
Phone		Email	

Class Name		Date	/ /
Name			
Address			
Phone		Email	

Class Name		Date	/ /
Name			
Address			
Phone		Email	

Classmates Log

Class Name		Date	/ /
Name			
Address			
Phone		Email	

Class Name		Date	/ /
Name			
Address			
Phone		Email	

Class Name		Date	/ /
Name			
Address			
Phone		Email	

Class Name		Date	/ /
Name			
Address			
Phone		Email	

Class Name		Date	/ /
Name			
Address			
Phone		Email	

Class Name		Date	/ /
Name			
Address			
Phone		Email	

Class Name		Date	/ /
Name			
Address			
Phone		Email	

Classmates Log

Class Name		Date	/ /
Name			
Address			
Phone		Email	

Class Name		Date	/ /
Name			
Address			
Phone		Email	

Class Name		Date	/ /
Name			
Address			
Phone		Email	

Class Name		Date	/ /
Name			
Address			
Phone		Email	

Class Name		Date	/ /
Name			
Address			
Phone		Email	

Class Name		Date	/ /
Name			
Address			
Phone		Email	

Class Name		Date	/ /
Name			
Address			
Phone		Email	

Classmates Log

Class Name		Date	/ /
Name			
Address			
Phone		Email	

Class Name		Date	/ /
Name			
Address			
Phone		Email	

Class Name		Date	/ /
Name			
Address			
Phone		Email	

Class Name		Date	/ /
Name			
Address			
Phone		Email	

Class Name		Date	/ /
Name			
Address			
Phone		Email	

Class Name		Date	/ /
Name			
Address			
Phone		Email	

Class Name		Date	/ /
Name			
Address			
Phone		Email	

Classmates Log

Class Name		Date	/ /
Name			
Address			
Phone		Email	

Class Name		Date	/ /
Name			
Address			
Phone		Email	

Class Name		Date	/ /
Name			
Address			
Phone		Email	

Class Name		Date	/ /
Name			
Address			
Phone		Email	

Class Name		Date	/ /
Name			
Address			
Phone		Email	

Class Name		Date	/ /
Name			
Address			
Phone		Email	

Class Name		Date	/ /
Name			
Address			
Phone		Email	

Classmates Log

Class Name		Date	/ /
Name			
Address			
Phone		Email	

Class Name		Date	/ /
Name			
Address			
Phone		Email	

Class Name		Date	/ /
Name			
Address			
Phone		Email	

Class Name		Date	/ /
Name			
Address			
Phone		Email	

Class Name		Date	/ /
Name			
Address			
Phone		Email	

Class Name		Date	/ /
Name			
Address			
Phone		Email	

Class Name		Date	/ /
Name			
Address			
Phone		Email	

Classmates Log

Class Name		Date	/ /
Name			
Address			
Phone		Email	

Class Name		Date	/ /
Name			
Address			
Phone		Email	

Class Name		Date	/ /
Name			
Address			
Phone		Email	

Class Name		Date	/ /
Name			
Address			
Phone		Email	

Class Name		Date	/ /
Name			
Address			
Phone		Email	

Class Name		Date	/ /
Name			
Address			
Phone		Email	

Class Name		Date	/ /
Name			
Address			
Phone		Email	

Classmates Log

Class Name		Date	/ /
Name			
Address			
Phone		Email	

Class Name		Date	/ /
Name			
Address			
Phone		Email	

Class Name		Date	/ /
Name			
Address			
Phone		Email	

Class Name		Date	/ /
Name			
Address			
Phone		Email	

Class Name		Date	/ /
Name			
Address			
Phone		Email	

Class Name		Date	/ /
Name			
Address			
Phone		Email	

Class Name		Date	/ /
Name			
Address			
Phone		Email	

Classmates Log

Class Name		Date	/ /
Name			
Address			
Phone		Email	

Class Name		Date	/ /
Name			
Address			
Phone		Email	

Class Name		Date	/ /
Name			
Address			
Phone		Email	

Class Name		Date	/ /
Name			
Address			
Phone		Email	

Class Name		Date	/ /
Name			
Address			
Phone		Email	

Class Name		Date	/ /
Name			
Address			
Phone		Email	

Class Name		Date	/ /
Name			
Address			
Phone		Email	

Classmates Log

Class Name		Date	/ /
Name			
Address			
Phone		Email	

Class Name		Date	/ /
Name			
Address			
Phone		Email	

Class Name		Date	/ /
Name			
Address			
Phone		Email	

Class Name		Date	/ /
Name			
Address			
Phone		Email	

Class Name		Date	/ /
Name			
Address			
Phone		Email	

Class Name		Date	/ /
Name			
Address			
Phone		Email	

Class Name		Date	/ /
Name			
Address			
Phone		Email	

References Log

Name	
Address	
Phone	Email

Name	
Address	
Phone	Email

Name	
Address	
Phone	Email

Name	
Address	
Phone	Email

Name	
Address	
Phone	Email

Name	
Address	
Phone	Email

Name	
Address	
Phone	Email

Name	
Address	
Phone	Email

Name	
Address	
Phone	Email

References Log

Name	
Address	
Phone		Email	

Name	
Address	
Phone		Email	

Name	
Address	
Phone		Email	

Name	
Address	
Phone		Email	

Name	
Address	
Phone		Email	

Name	
Address	
Phone		Email	

Name	
Address	
Phone		Email	

Name	
Address	
Phone		Email	

Name	
Address	
Phone		Email	

References Log

Name	
Address	
Phone	Email

Name	
Address	
Phone	Email

Name	
Address	
Phone	Email

Name	
Address	
Phone	Email

Name	
Address	
Phone	Email

Name	
Address	
Phone	Email

Name	
Address	
Phone	Email

Name	
Address	
Phone	Email

Name	
Address	
Phone	Email

References Log

Name	
Address	
Phone	Email

Name	
Address	
Phone	Email

Name	
Address	
Phone	Email

Name	
Address	
Phone	Email

Name	
Address	
Phone	Email

Name	
Address	
Phone	Email

Name	
Address	
Phone	Email

Name	
Address	
Phone	Email

Name	
Address	
Phone	Email

References Log

Name	
Address	
Phone	Email

Name	
Address	
Phone	Email

Name	
Address	
Phone	Email

Name	
Address	
Phone	Email

Name	
Address	
Phone	Email

Name	
Address	
Phone	Email

Name	
Address	
Phone	Email

Name	
Address	
Phone	Email

Name	
Address	
Phone	Email

References Log

Name	
Address	
Phone	Email

Name	
Address	
Phone	Email

Name	
Address	
Phone	Email

Name	
Address	
Phone	Email

Name	
Address	
Phone	Email

Name	
Address	
Phone	Email

Name	
Address	
Phone	Email

Name	
Address	
Phone	Email

Name	
Address	
Phone	Email

References Log

Name	
Address	
Phone	Email

Name	
Address	
Phone	Email

Name	
Address	
Phone	Email

Name	
Address	
Phone	Email

Name	
Address	
Phone	Email

Name	
Address	
Phone	Email

Name	
Address	
Phone	Email

Name	
Address	
Phone	Email

Name	
Address	
Phone	Email

References Log

Name	
Address	
Phone	Email

Name	
Address	
Phone	Email

Name	
Address	
Phone	Email

Name	
Address	
Phone	Email

Name	
Address	
Phone	Email

Name	
Address	
Phone	Email

Name	
Address	
Phone	Email

Name	
Address	
Phone	Email

Name	
Address	
Phone	Email

References Log

Name	
Address	
Phone	Email

Name	
Address	
Phone	Email

Name	
Address	
Phone	Email

Name	
Address	
Phone	Email

Name	
Address	
Phone	Email

Name	
Address	
Phone	Email

Name	
Address	
Phone	Email

Name	
Address	
Phone	Email

Name	
Address	
Phone	Email

References Log

Name	
Address	
Phone		Email	

Name	
Address	
Phone		Email	

Name	
Address	
Phone		Email	

Name	
Address	
Phone		Email	

Name	
Address	
Phone		Email	

Name	
Address	
Phone		Email	

Name	
Address	
Phone		Email	

Name	
Address	
Phone		Email	

Name	
Address	
Phone		Email	

Instructions

Your *ZuluShield Logbook / Reload* is the most vital ingredient of any Firearms Legal Defense. Utilize your *ZuluShield Logbook / Reload* to document important data about individual training events, licenses certificates, literary facts; such as news articles related to Firearms Self-Defense or Use-of-Force, personal notes, contact information and more.

Whether you've participated in a high speed run and gun course, a *ZuluFight* session at home or read an interesting article or book about a real-world incident, *ZuluShield* can translate this information into a completely customized, bulletproof Firearms Legal Defense. If used appropriately, this system will will be your life-line when it comes time to recall specific facts about your training history, highlight your dedication, professionalism and competence, as well as being the one-stop-evidence-source to aid in your actual Legal Defense. With *ZuluShield* you'll have what you need to win both the battle and the war.

Remember, consistency in documentation is just as important as consistency with your weapon.

- Your *ZuluShield Logbook / Reload* should be treated as *"Documentary Evidence"* for Legal Defense purposes. With this in mind, keep accurate, consistent and neat data with 'Court Appropriate' language.

- Stay consistent! Documenting your training and other information only takes a few minutes. When you're facing a Criminal or Civil Self-Defense proceeding tomorrow, you'll be VERY thankful you wisely invested your time today.

- It is highly suggested that you use a mechanical pencil as opposed to an ink pen, when inputting information *ZuluShield* logs. Mechanical pencils are inexpensive, more reliable, neater, mistake proof and capable of very fine writing, which allows for adequate space within data fields.

- Over the years you're likely to accumulate a number of *ZuluShield Logbooks / Reloads.* Be sure to dedicate a safe and secure location to store <u>ALL</u> your *ZuluShield* products. The IRS may audit you for 7 years, however this information will prove to be vital to your Legal Defense even decades from now. Make sure to retain <u>ALL</u> your *ZuluShield* products <u>INDEFINITELY</u>.

Reload:

It's extremely important that you stick with this system and purchase *Reloads* as you run out of available logs. Reloads can be found at *www.zulutactical.com/zulushield* or by using the QR Code on on Page (284).

Legal Notice:

On Page (1) you will find a legal noticed titled 'ATTENTION!!!'

1. It's imperative that you read this notice in its entirety.

2. Then sign and print your legal name.

The intent of this notice is to notify law enforcement officers that the material and information related to this system is your own private communication and is 'Protected Matter' which shall not be seized.

Cover Page:

On the bottom of Page (3), you'll find a table for inputting your information. This is critical, <u>DON'T SKIP THIS</u>. This will marry this particular *ZuluShield* product to you. Remember *ZuluShield* is your 'Attorney Communiqué' and needs to be yours and yours alone in order for it to be considered 'Protected Communication'.

1. Input your full legal name.

2. Now input which Book Number this book represents in its chronology with your previous *ZuluShield* products. The main *ZuluShield* chapter book is always Book Number (1).

3. Next input your mailing address should this book be lost.

4. After that input your contact phone number.

5. Finally input your email address.

Licenses Logs:

Beginning from Page (83) you'll find (5) different types of License Logs. The first (4); Concealed Carry List, Open Carry List, Assault Weapons List and the Unrestricted Magazine List, are intended to be used for future quick-reference should you end up traveling with your firearms. The final log, the 'Licenses Log' is where you'll input each individual license you hold.

Concealed Carry List:

1. Determine which States offer 'Reciprocity' with your particular Concealed Weapons License. Both Google and UsaCarry.com are great recourses in finding this out.

2. Place an (x) beside each State and or Territory you're authorized to Concealed Carry in.

3. Always remember that even if an outside State offers reciprocity, they may require you to first apply for their State's carry license prior to you actually carrying in their State.

4. It's not uncommon for States to change their laws so it's important to update this list every six months and confirm that your list is still accurate.

5. Refer to this list whenever you're planning on traveling with your firearm to assure you're 100% certain exactly where you're covered.

Open Carry List:

1. Determine which States offer 'Open Carry'. Both Google and UsaCarry.com are great recourses in finding this out.

2. Place an (x) beside each State and or Territory you're authorized to Open Carry in.

3. Keep in mind that although a 'State' may authorize this form of carry, some cities and municipals within that State may not.

4. It's not uncommon for States to change their laws so it's important to update this list every six months and confirm that your list is still accurate.

5. Refer to this list whenever you're planning on traveling with your firearm to assure you're 100% certain exactly where you're covered.

Assault Weapons List:

1. Determine which States allow 'Assault Weapons' & Full-Auto weapons. Google is a great recourse in finding this out.

2. Place an (x) beside each State and or Territory which authorize these types of weapons.

3. Keep in mind that although a 'State' may authorize these kinds of weapons, some cities and municipals within that State may not.

4. It's not uncommon for States to change their laws so it's important to update this list every six months and confirm that your list is still accurate.

5. Refer to this list whenever you're planning on traveling with your firearm to assure you're 100% certain exactly where you're covered.

Unrestricted Magazines List:

1. Determine which States allow 'Unrestricted Magazines'. Google is a great recourse in finding this out.

2. Place an (x) beside each State and or Territory which authorize these types of magazines.

3. Keep in mind that although a 'State' may authorize these kinds of magazines, some cities and municipals within that State may not.

4. It's not uncommon for States to change their laws so it's important to update this list every six months and confirm that your list is still accurate.

5. Refer to this list whenever you're planning on traveling with your firearm to assure you're 100% certain exactly where you're covered.

Licenses Log:

1. Input the 'Title' or type of license.

2. Input the date your license was issued.

3. If applicable, input the date your license expires. If not input an "N/A"

4. If you intend to carry the license on your person, take a photo copy of the license and file that copy in your *ZuluShield Archive* in the 'Certificates Section'.

5. If you do not intend to carry your license on your person, file the original license in the 'Licenses Section' of your *ZuluShield Archive*.

Certificates Logs:

Beginning from Page (91) you'll find 'Certificate Logs' where you'll input each individual certificate you hold.

1. Input the 'Title' or type of certificate.

2. If applicable, input the instructor who issued the certificate. If not input an "N/A"

3. If applicable, input the issuing entity who issued the certificate. If not input an "N/A"

4. Now input the date your certificate was issued.

5. File the original certificate in the 'Certificates Section' of your *ZuluShield Archive*.

Training Logs:

Beginning from Page (97) you'll find 'Training Logs' where you'll input each individual training session you participate in.

1. Input the date you participated in the training.

2. Next input the time you participated in the training.

3. Now input what type of training, i.e. *ZuluFight*, course, conference.

4. If applicable, input the name of the company who gave the training.

5. If applicable, input the instructor who conducted the training. If not applicable input an "N/A".

6. If applicable, input the contact information of the company and instructor who conducted the training. If not input an "N/A"

7. Now indicate if this training was certified meaning you received an actual certificate by circling 'Yes' or 'No'.

8. If applicable, input the course fee or cost. If not input an "N/A"

9. Next input the duration of this training session. Remember to be specific. Make sure to indicate if the unit of measurement is 'Minutes' or 'Hours' so there's no confusion later.

10. Lastly, the 'Notes' field is intended to allow you to document whatever information you believe is important for future reference. Describe the training event, what you learned and how it relates to your future Defense. If you completed a *ZuluFight* session, be specific and indicate which positions you focused on and how things went. Remember to input important 'Waypoints' of information that can easily remind you of the actual training even years down the road.

11. Should you require more room for notes, draft an actual report. You might even prefer to make a digital copy of your report via PDF or scanner. Either way you'll want to indicate this in the 'Notes Section' of the Training Log, then retain this file in the 'Training Section' of your *ZuluShield Archive* or *Zdrive*.

12. Always remember to duplicate <u>EVERY</u> file on your *Zdrive*, by creating a duplicate on your back-up *Zdrive*.

Literary Logs:

Beginning from Page (149) you'll find 'Literary Logs' where you'll input each literary items you believe to be important to your Legal Defense.

1. Input the *Topic* which this particular item refers to.

2. Now input the *Title* or head of this particular item.

3. If applicable, input the *Author*, if not input an "N/A"

4. Next input the date you read this information.

5. The *Summary Section* is intended for you to give a brief summary of the item as a quick-reference to quickly jog your member.

6. Now compose your report. You might even prefer to make a digital copy of this file via PDF or scanner. Either way you'll want to retain this file in the 'Literary Section' of your *ZuluShield Archive* or *Zdrive*.

7. Always remember to duplicate <u>EVERY</u> file on your *Zdrive*, by creating a duplicate on your back-up *Zdrive*.

Multi-Media Logs:

Beginning from Page (177) you'll find 'Multi-Media Logs' where you'll input each multi-media related items you believe to be important to your Legal Defense.

1. Input the *Topic* which this particular item refers to.

2. Now input the *Title* or head of this particular item.

3. Next input the *Source* where you found this item.

4. Now input the *Date* you viewed this information.

5. The *Summary Section* is intended for you to give a brief summary of the item as a quick-reference to quickly jog your member.

6. Now it's time to compose a report about the information. You might even prefer to make a digital copy of this report via PDF or scanner. Either way you'll want to retain this file in the 'Multi-Media Section' of your *ZuluShield Archive* or *Zdrive*.

7. Don't forget to also download your Multi-Media file to your *Zdrive*.

8. Always remember to duplicate <u>EVERY</u> file on your *Zdrive*, by creating a duplicate on your back-up *Zdrive*.

Notes Logs:

Beginning from Page (207) you'll find 'Notes Logs' where you'll document particular reports you compose on items you believe to be important to your Legal Defense.

1. Input the *Topic* which this particular item refers to.

2. Next input the *Date* you composed this report.

3. If applicable, input the *Title* or heading of this particular item. If not applicable input an "N/A".

4. If applicable, input the *Source*. If not applicable input an "N/A".

5. The *Summary Section* is intended for you to give a brief summary of the report as a quick-reference to quickly jog your member.

6. Now it's time to file your report. You might even prefer to make a digital copy of this file via PDF or scanner. Either way you'll want to retain this file in the 'Notes Section' of your *ZuluShield Archive* or *Zdrive*.

7. Always remember to duplicate <u>EVERY</u> file on your *Zdrive*, by creating a duplicate on your back-up *Zdrive*.

Contacts Logs:

Beginning from Page (235) you'll find (4) different types of Contacts Logs. The intent of the logs is to provide you with a surplus of viable point of contact which will weigh heavily on your ability to initiate your Legal Defense when the time comes.

Attorneys Log:

1. Input the attorney's *Name*.

2. Now indicate their *Specialty* i.e. Criminal Self-Defense, Civil Self-Defense and so on.

3. Input the name of their *Company* or practice.

4. Now input the *Address* where they can be located.

5. Next input their contact *Phone* number.

6. Lastly, find their *Email* address and input that.

Experts Log:

1. Input the expert's *Name*.

2. Now indicate their *Specialty* i.e. Firearms Instructor, Force Science Expert and so on.

3. Input the name of their *Company*.

4. Now input the *Address* where they can be located.

5. Next input their contact *Phone* number.

6. Lastly, find their *Email* address and input that.

Classmates Log:

1. Input the *Class Name*.

2. Next input the *Date* you attended the class.

3. Now input the classmate's *Name*.

4. Next input their mailing *Address*.

5. Next input their contact *Phone* number.

6. Lastly, input their *Email* address.

References Log:

1. Input your reference's *Name*.

2. Next input their mailing *Address*.

3. Next input their contact *Phone* number.

4. Lastly, input their *Email* address.

ZuluShield:

Whether you're in need of a Reload or maybe a gift for a friend or family member, getting another copy couldn't be easier. Use the QR Code to the right or visit our website today!

zulutactical.com/zulushield

ZuluFight:

Whether you're in need of a replacement or maybe a gift for a friend or family member, getting another copy couldn't be easier. Use the QR Code to the right or visit our website today!

zulutactical.com/zulufight

TeamZulu:

Stay up to date with all things *ZULU*. Connect with us on Facebook. Learn why fans from around the World choose *ZULU*. Use the QR Code to the right or visit our website today!

facebook.com/zulutac

Disclaimer

By using the ZuluShield System, the user assumes sole responsibility and liability. It is the sole responsibility and liability of the user to honestly and accurately document and retain the appropriate information and exhibits for Legal Defense purposes. It is the sole responsibility and liability of the user to update this information and to safety store this system for future use. Zulu Tactical LLC assumes no responsibility or liability whatsoever for any damage or loss and or theft of any component of this system or the information stored within this system. The user understands items and information retained in this system are generally made of paper, which is susceptible to damage due to moisture, humidity and heat. Exposure to moisture, humidity and heat may cause this system's components to deteriorate over time. The user assumes sole responsibility and liability for maintaining the longevity and integrity of this system. Zulu Tactical LLC assumes no responsibility or liability whatsoever for the use of this system or for its usefulness during legal proceedings. The user understands legal proceedings are complicated and unique to each individual and understands that any legal proceeding's outcome is completely depended upon the totality of the circumstances related to the incidents for which the proceedings specifically address. The primary function of the ZuluShield System is to provide a practical and organized means of collecting, documenting and retaining vital information, which is then used to communicate this data to their attorney for Legal Defense purposes. The ZuluShield System is not guaranteed to produce a legal victory. It's intended to be utilized as a 'Good Faith' effort in providing an organized and detailed blueprint of an individual's training, proficiency and understanding of the totality of the circumstances related to the subject of Firearms Self-Defense.